DEFIANT

DEFIANT

GROWING UP IN THE JIM CROW SOUTH

WADE HUDSON

CROWN BOOKS FOR YOUNG READERS
NEW YORK

To my wife, Cheryl; daughter, Katura; son, Stephan;
the Hudson clan; and those who came before and
helped to pave the way. I shall forever remember!

Text copyright © 2021 by Wade Hudson
Jacket art copyright © 2021 by Charly Palmer

Visit us on the Web! rhcbooks.com

Educators and librarians, for a variety of teaching tools, visit us at
RHTeachersLibrarians.com

Library of Congress Cataloging-in-Publication Data
Names: Hudson, Wade, author.
Title: Defiant: growing up in the Jim Crow South / Wade Hudson.
Other titles: Growing up in the Jim Crow South
Description: New York: Crown Books for Young Readers, [2021] |
Includes bibliographical references. | Audience: Ages 10+ | Audience: Grades 4–6 |
Summary: "The memoir of Wade Hudson, a Black man and Civil Rights activist who came
of age in the 1960s at the height of the Civil Rights Movement"—Provided by publisher.
Identifiers: LCCN 2021021762 (print) | LCCN 2021021763 (ebook) |
ISBN 978-0-593-12635-6 (hardcover) | ISBN 978-0-593-12636-3 (library binding) |
ISBN 978-0-593-12637-0 (ebook)
Subjects: LCSH: Hudson, Wade—Juvenile literature. | Civil rights workers—Louisiana—
Biography—Juvenile literature. | African American boys—Louisiana—Biography—
Juvenile literature. | African Americans—Louisiana—Social life and customs—
20th century—Juvenile literature. | Civil rights movements—United States—
Juvenile literature. | Coming of age—Juvenile literature. | Mansfield (La.)—
Biography—Juvenile literature.
Classification: LCC F376.3.H83 A3 2021 (print) | LCC F376.3.H83 (ebook) |
DDC 323.092 [B]—dc23

The text of this book is set in 11.2-point Gamma ITC Std.
Interior design by Cathy Bobak

Printed in the United States of America
10 9 8 7 6 5 4 3 2 1
First Edition

Random House Children's Books supports the First Amendment
and celebrates the right to read.

CONTENTS

DEFIANT DREAMS

Dream bold and brave.
Dream what goes beyond your reach,
And ask those tough questions
In search of a redefined future.

Do not dream the routine dreams.
Dreams that conform to what others accept,
That yield to what seeks to box you in,
That limit your reach and determine your
    destiny.

Dream dreams like those that created the pyramids,
That constructed Great Zimbabwe,
That put Phillis Wheatley's pen to paper,
That gave birth to *Freedom's Journal.*

Dreams that inspired Harriet to free the enslaved,
That built Tuskegee, Spelman, and Bethune-
    Cookman,
That impelled Garvey to declare "Rise Up!"
That stare reality in the eyes and do not blink.

Dream like Dr. Martin Luther King Jr.,
Like Sojourner Truth, Frederick Douglass, and
    Malcolm X,
Like those who started Black Lives Matter,
Who would not be held back.

Dream dreams that confront hatred and injustice,
That respond to those crying out in the darkness,
That plant you firmly on the community
    watchtower,
Ever vigilant, ever protective.

Dream what is not always easy to achieve,
What is sometimes feisty and defiant,
What seeks to plant the fertile seeds of change,
And yearns to help set people free.

Dream dreams like those bold ones that came
    before,
That were wrapped in love and baptized in
    courage,
That faced the mightiest challenges,
Determined to create a better world!

PREFACE

During school visits and other presentations, I often share stories about what it was like being a Black youngster in the 1950s and 1960s, during a pivotal time in our nation's history. Many students know little about this period. Some have been introduced to Dr. Martin Luther King Jr.'s "I Have a Dream" speech or Rosa Parks's refusal to give up her seat on a Montgomery, Alabama, bus. They are always intrigued to hear what it was like to be a kid during Jim Crow. I never, however, considered sharing these stories—my story—in a book.

In the summer of 2018, at an American Library Association convention, my wife, Cheryl, and I were promoting *We Rise, We Resist, We Raise Our Voices,* an anthology we had edited. During the luncheon with members of the publisher's staff, I shared stories about my experiences in the South. Someone suggested that I write a memoir. Others seconded the suggestion, repeating how important it would be to present my story to young readers.

For the first time, I gave writing my memoir serious consideration. Was I ready to dive into the past and shine a light on those experiences that shaped and molded me? Was I ready to relive the pain that remembering past incidents would surely kindle? Was I ready to spotlight my parents and my siblings in all their completeness? Was I ready to force onstage, for others to see, the people I knew and loved and who played significant roles in my growth? Was I ready to share myself?

When I was made a formal offer by Crown, I accepted. In doing so, I also accepted the challenge to write my story and introduce the world to my hometown, Mansfield, Louisiana, and its people and those who were a part of my coming-of-age journey.

Writing this memoir has been a provocative yet fulfilling project. I have learned so much more about the town in which I grew up. I have gained a better perspective of the Black people of Mansfield and the lives they lived. It is a perspective that reveals just how creative, resilient, dedicated, tough, and loving they were. To endure a system that was devised to dehumanize them and, in some instances, destroy them, they had to be.

After completing the manuscript for *Defiant,* I discovered a story about a group of brave Black folks in Mansfield who struggled to register to vote in the mid 1950s. Led by Thomas Louis White Sr., the group endured the usual demeaning epithets and threats Black people often faced, especially those who dared to speak up for their rights. The registrar, who was White, of course, used every means that the brutal, racist system afforded to stop them from registering. But Thomas White and his group were determined. Risking their livelihoods and their lives, they came back again and again. Finally, the registrar relented and allowed some in their group, including Thomas White, to register. They were among the first Blacks to vote in Mansfield. Perhaps the registrar didn't see several Blacks participating in the political process as a threat.

I never knew about this story when I was growing up. I don't recall anyone in the community talking about it. In fact, I didn't think there were any Black voters in Mansfield. I am sure there are other stories like this, of resistance and standing up for rights, that are hidden from history just as the Tulsa Race Massacre was hidden from history for so many decades.

I have learned about myself, my motivations, my inspirations, and in many ways, my raison d'être. I have learned how much I am a part of those people from Mansfield, Louisiana, and how much they are a part of me. *Defiant: Growing Up in the Jim Crow South* is my story, but it is their story, too. I hope I have done it justice!

CHAPTER 1

Civil Rights and Protests

So this is what solitary confinement is like? I asked myself, shaking my head.

There was no one else in the tiny eight-foot-by-eight-foot cell to hear me. A small sink near a toilet stood out. There were no windows. A thin mattress with a sheet and a blanket thrown over it rested on the concrete floor. There was no pillow.

I had thought the dormitory rooms on the campus of Southern University, the institution that I attended, were small. They now seemed like large suites at the Waldorf Astoria in New York City compared to this suffocating place.

I sat down on the mattress and leaned against the brick wall. I didn't know what was happening. Why had a warrant been issued for *my* arrest? I hadn't done anything illegal!

A little more than an hour earlier, I had been in a car with two friends, on our way to a grocery store. With the windows rolled down, we were enjoying the nice spring breeze that blew into the car and cooled us off. The latest R & B hits played loudly on the radio. Suddenly, a news flash interrupted our groove and caught our attention.

> Two Negro men were arrested this morning in the Scotlandville section of Baton Rouge. They have been identified as Alphonse Snedecor and Frank A. Stewart. Both men are wanted for conspiracy to murder Baton Rouge mayor Woody Dumas and a number of other city officials, authorities said. A press conference will be held later today, when more details will be disclosed. A third man identified as Wade Hudson is being sought, authorities added. Both Stewart and Hudson are leaders of SOUL, a civil rights organization with headquarters in the Scotlandville section of Baton Rouge. Snedecor, a Baton Rouge native, is also a member of the group.

No one said a word as the music began to play again. It was as if the world had stopped.

James Holden, Stewart's cousin and the owner and driver of the car we were riding in, slammed his open hand hard against the steering wheel.

"What the . . . !" He didn't finish the sentence.

"Damn! Damn! They must have picked up Frank just after we left. This is bad."

"Who else they gonna arrest?" Barbara George, the third member of our trio, asked. The fear in her voice was apparent.

I didn't say anything. Staring at nothing in particular, I began thinking about all the other young Black freedom fighters around the country who had been arrested or killed. I had even donated to fundraising efforts for many of them. I thought about Fred Hampton and Mark Clark, Black Panther leaders who had been killed a few months earlier by the police in Chicago. Would Frank, Alphonse, or I become three more casualties?

"Holden! Take me to the bus station," I blurted. "I gotta get out of Dodge, man! I gotta get out of town. These folks will either kill me or send me to prison for the rest of my life. I got to get out of here!"

Holden pulled over to the side of the road and stopped the car. He and Barbara looked at me.

"That's what you want to do?" Holden asked pointedly.

"Yeah, man, I'm splitting! These are crazy White folks! I don't know what they'll do. You heard what the man said on the radio. They're accusing us of trying to kill the mayor and some other White officials."

"But you can't go to the bus station," Barbara interjected. "Cops are probably there, too, and at the airport."

"Well, drop me off at the bus station in Cheneyville or some other town not too far from here. I ain't going to jail for the rest of my life!"

I looked around, now concerned that the police might be closing in on us.

"Wade, if you run and they catch up with you, they'll shoot you. I'm telling you. They'll shoot you."

"Barbara is right," Holden added. "They already got Frank and Alphonse. If they do catch you, it'll just look like you're guilty. Frank ain't guilty. He wouldn't hurt a fly."

"That don't matter!" I shot back quickly. "They're just trying to get us out of the way. They're trying to kill the organization. They've been doing this across the country. We've been pushing voter registration and trying to get Black people to vote. If more Black people vote, we can get these White, racist politicians out of office, and they know that. They don't want Black people to have any power."

Frank Stewart and I, along with a small group of other community activists who were mostly students at Southern University, had formed the organization we named the Society for Opportunity, Unity, and Leadership. Its primary purpose was to deal with conditions in the Black community caused principally by racism and discrimination. We called the group SOUL. Barbara was a member. A veteran of the Vietnam War, Alphonse had joined, too.

SOUL had started a breakfast program to feed hungry kids, established a small library of Black books, and conducted rap sessions where conditions in the all-Black Scotlandville neighborhood were discussed. We were beginning to move into the political arena, too, encouraging people to vote. Some of our members had begun wearing berets, like the Black Panthers did.

"I think you should turn yourself in so y'all can fight this together," Barbara suggested.

"What?! Turn myself in? You got to be kidding, Barbara! Man, this is crazy." I forced a laugh, but the situation wasn't funny. It wasn't funny at all.

"Even if you're able to get away and make it out of the country, you won't be able to come back."

I thought about what Barbara had said. If I couldn't come back, that would mean I wouldn't be able to see my family anymore, or all the people I knew and loved.

"You think I should turn myself in, too?" I asked Holden.

"It's better than being dead! These White folks will shoot you!"

I let out a chestful of air. As the three of us sat there in that car for what seemed like forever, I considered next steps. It all seemed so surreal. No, unreal. I'd known this could happen, that what we called the racist White power structure in Baton Rouge could pounce on us one day. The truth was, we were fortunate it hadn't happened sooner.

"Y'all really feel I should turn myself in?" I asked again, seeking assurance.

Neither Barbara nor Holden answered. The looks on their faces said it all.

"Okay! Let's do it! Let's get it over with!"

The music, now at a lower volume, played in the background as the car moved slowly toward downtown Baton Rouge.

"I've never seen you drive this slow, Holden. You scared?"

"You damn right!" He laughed and said, "You don't want

them to stop this car and pick you up before you can turn yourself in, do you?"

The parking area at the East Baton Rouge Parish Sheriff's Office was packed, but we found a spot. After walking into the building, we headed for the counter where a heavyset White man in uniform sat. I stepped forward.

"Can I help y'all?" the officer asked in his Southern drawl without looking up from his notepad.

I looked at Barbara and at Holden, then turned to face the officer again.

"I'm Wade Hudson," I told him.

"So?" he responded condescendingly.

"I understand there's a warrant out for my arrest. Hudson, Wade Hudson." I repeated my name.

My name finally registered with him. He jumped up from his chair and called several other officers over.

"This is the third one," he told them.

The officers pushed me against the counter, forced my arms behind my back, and handcuffed me. As they led me away, I looked back at Barbara and Holden just in time to see Holden thrust a raised fist into the air.

"We'll get a lawyer for you, Wade!" Barbara said. "Hang in there."

After being fingerprinted and photographed for a mug shot for the first time in my life, I was taken to this small cell in the basement of the jail.

Since my incarceration began, I hadn't seen anyone except

police officers and several detectives who came to stare at me through a small window in the door of my cell. I knew nothing about the charges I was being held on. I was completely in the dark.

The brick wall that I was resting my head against started to give me a headache. I decided to try the thin mattress, but it wasn't much better.

I couldn't help but wonder whether this was the end for me. Conspiracy to murder the mayor and who knew who else? How could I ever get out of a fabricated frame-up like this?

It had been a little more than five years since I'd left my home in Mansfield to attend Southern University. It seemed so much longer. A lot had happened during those years.

At home when I was growing up, I had followed the civil rights movement and the events that unfolded in the South and around the country. I wanted to be involved. I wanted to make my own contribution, take my stand for freedom, just as Dr. Martin Luther King Jr., John Lewis, Daisy Bates, Stokely Carmichael, and Rosa Parks were doing. I yearned for the opportunity to confront the evils of Jim Crow segregation that forced the people I knew and loved to be subservient to White people.

Mansfield, however, was like thousands of other small rural towns across the South that White people controlled virtually unimpeded. Fighting against their system of oppression often resulted in lost jobs, being run out of town, or, worse, being killed. These were enormous prices to pay. But I wanted to fight back; I burned to do something about the evil that haunted my people.

So, you might say that my experiences in Mansfield led me to this place. How I grew up there, how those impactful years shaped me, all pointed me toward a future I had to embrace. Even if it led me to jail.

CHAPTER 2

The Mary Street Boys

"Run, Ray. Run!" I yelled, backpedaling, clutching the football in my small right hand.

Ray darted down the field and I threw the ball as far as I could. It reached his hands while he was in stride.

But he dropped it! The ball was right in his hands and he dropped it!

One big, unified groan from our team greeted the miscue.

"That was a touchdown, Ray! You dropped a touchdown!" PG cried out.

"What's wrong with you, boy?" Crow complained. "We needed that score."

The opposing team broke out in loud clapping and back slapping.

"Ray can't catch a cold in the dead of winter," one of them joked. "He need some glue on his hands."

Acting cool, Ray shook his head, and walked back to our huddle.

"I'll get the next one," he proclaimed.

During afternoons and evenings when leaves had begun to fall, the hot summer days that folks complained about had gone, and a new school year had started, we could usually be found playing football on the large lawn at Mr. and Mrs. Blow's house. We were the boys who lived on or near Mary Street, one of the major roads that ran through the east side of Black Mansfield.

Mr. and Mrs. Blow's house was unlike the houses that dotted Mary Street. The remodeled brick structure stood out among the wooden dwellings. It looked more like the houses that had sprouted up in White suburbs across the country during the 1950s and 1960s. We saw them in popular magazines such as *Good Housekeeping* and *The Saturday Evening Post*. Black folks couldn't live in those White-only suburbs, but that didn't stop those who had the money from building their own suburban-looking homes. That's what Mr. and Mrs. Blow had done. They were both schoolteachers.

But it was the Blows' lawn that we cared most about. We claimed it as our own football field, wide and with a lot of space on which to run like a real one. We could throw long passes, cut across it to dodge tacklers, and even punt on fourth downs. The grass was bright green and deep like the carpeting in rich folks' homes. It was always neatly cut.

Determined to keep our games going, we sometimes played until it was so dark, we could barely see each other. Only Sundays were unavailable to us. Sunday was the Lord's Day.

Our group included my brother PG and other boys our ages, seven, eight, and nine years old.

In the fall and winter, we played football. When spring came, we turned to baseball and played until the weather started to change and football made its appearance again on television.

Our baseball games were played across the street from the Blows' house, directly in front of Ray Bogan's, on a vacant lot next to our other neighbors, Mr. Otis and Miss Ella Lee's house.

For all of us, football and baseball players were role models. In football, we idolized Jim Brown, Ollie Matson, Willie Galimore, Lenny Moore, and other Black players who had established successful careers in the sport. In baseball, it was Willie Mays, Hank Aaron, Ernie Banks, Don Newcombe, and Roy Campanella. They all had overcome racism and discrimination to play in the highest professional leagues in sports. Their exploits were featured in *Jet* and *Ebony* magazines, two national African American publications. They were in the sports pages of White newspapers that wouldn't cover any positive stories about other Black people. Even the daily newspapers in segregated Shreveport, the city north of Mansfield, covered them.

We saw our heroes on TV in the baseball game of the week on Saturdays and in football games on Sundays. We emulated them. We held our bats like Banks and tried to learn how to make the basket catch like Mays. We wanted to run over opposing players like Jimmy Brown and fake out tacklers like Lenny Moore.

Jackie Robinson was my father's hero. Whenever we raved about Mays or Aaron, he would say, "Jackie is the man." Robinson had made it possible for Black baseball players to play in the major leagues. His success paved the way for Black athletes in other sports, too. Many Black Americans idolized him for integrating baseball in 1947, when he took the field for the Brooklyn Dodgers. It was a feat bigger than when Joe Louis knocked out the German fighter Max Schmeling in 1938. Or when Jesse Owens won four gold medals at the 1936 Olympics. Black people celebrated those accomplishments, which brought honor not just to Black people but to the country.

Jackie, however, had to bring it day after day, game after game, at bat after at bat, facing racial taunts and physical abuse. Jackie had to deliver. Every time.

People followed his every game.

"How did Jackie do yesterday?"

"Did he get a hit today?"

"Did he steal a base?"

"Did a White player spike our boy Jackie?"

Jazz bandleader Buddy Johnson even wrote and recorded a song that extolled Jackie's achievements and illuminated his fame. "Did You See Jackie Robinson Hit That Ball?" reached number thirteen on the Billboard charts. Count Basie, a leading jazz composer and orchestra leader, also recorded the song, and his version became a baseball standard.

By the mid-1950s, when we were really old enough to appreciate his baseball skills, Jackie's most productive days were behind him. Rather than accept a trade from the Dodgers, the team he had helped to win six National League pennants in ten years, to the New York Giants, Jackie chose to retire. My father had tears in his eyes when he heard the news. He wasn't the only one.

For little Black boys in urban areas and in small country towns across the nation, Jackie showed us the way. We believed sports would offer us opportunities for a different and better future. We played the games for enjoyment, but we also played believing we could become the next Jackie Robinson, or the next Willie Mays or Jim Brown, or another Black sports hero.

On this day, as we continued playing our game, no one kept score. But we all knew in our heads the number of touchdowns each of us had made and how many tackles we had accumulated.

Then a booming voice stopped us in our tracks.

"Don't y'all hurt each other, now! I see you over there!"

It was my mother.

"If y'all don't play more careful, I'm gonna make all of you go home!"

From across the street, she had seen one of us being tackled hard to the ground. To her, we were hurting each other. Many times, PG and I came home after a game with battle scars proving we were worthy competitors. Madear didn't see it that way. Boys who were too rough had hurt her sons, she thought. She would threaten not to let us play anymore. But she never stopped us.

We all knew that if Madear told us to stop the game and go home, we had to do it. Almost all respected adults in our community had that kind of authority over us. You listened to older folks. You had better. If not, you would surely pay the price. That price usually was a whipping or having a privilege, such as playing football or baseball, taken away for a period of time.

"Be cool, Miss Leen. We ain't gonna get hurt," Cleonis yelled back politely.

My mother's name was Lurline. But people in Mansfield shortened names or came up with nicknames. The oldest girl in a family was called Sister. The oldest son? Well, Brother, of course. That was the nickname my family gave me. I was the oldest son in my family. My brother Willis Fred was PG, and Wilbert Charles, another brother, was called Lillo. Our youngest brother, Major, was Babebro. Being called by one's birth name was rare. So the youngsters in the neighborhood dropped the Lur in my mother's first name and just called her Miss Leen. But we, her children, called her Madear.

"This is how you play football, Miss Leen." Crow spoke up as we got ready to run another play. PG and I didn't say a word. We understood the wisdom of silence, at least in this situation.

"I don't care how you play football," Madear shot back

without hesitation. "If you get hurt, you hurt. Y'all better be careful like I told ya!"

I got the ball and dodged two would-be tacklers but couldn't avoid another. He slammed me to the ground and others piled on top. After the boys pulled themselves up, I rose slowly, afraid Madear had seen the play. I glanced toward our front yard, expecting to see her standing with both hands resting on her hips. I breathed a sigh of relief when I saw she wasn't there, thankful she hadn't seen me at the bottom of the pile. I know Madear would have walked over, marched PG and me home, and made the others go home, too.

We began to smell the aromas of various foods cooking at houses all along the street. Collard greens, fried chicken, candied sweet potatoes, corn bread, and pork chops beckoned us.

"Man, that food sho' smell good," Ray Bogan said, stopping to take a big whiff. "I bet my grandma's cooking them greens."

"How you know it's your grandma?" Cleonis jumped in. "It could be Miss Leen cookin' them greens."

"I know how my grandma's greens smell," Ray shot back.

"Boy, you crazy. You sayin' your grandma's greens got a special smell?"

"Yeah, they do. I know how she fix 'em."

We all laughed at the exchange between Cleonis and Ray. But our game continued. Crow caught a pass and someone tripped him as he streaked up the field. When he landed, his head hit the ground hard. He rose, mumbling incoherently, and staggered back to the huddle.

"Crow out cold on his feet! Look at him," someone yelled, laughing.

"You all right, Crow?" I asked as he stood next to me in the huddle.

"I'm okay. I'm ready for the next play."

Then we heard that loud, roaring voice from across the street again.

"All y'all go home to eat! It's time to eat! Brother, you and PG come on! Food's on the table! Your daddy will be home from work soon!"

With that pronouncement, our game officially ended. We made sure Crow was all right and headed to our homes. Dinner was an exclamation mark at the end of another typical day for us, the Mary Street Boys.

CHAPTER 3

The Beginning

My father was born and raised in Louisiana, the second oldest of four brothers and a sister. His mother, Geneva Johnson, had been married twice. The father of her first three children was Major Hudson, my father's father. The other children were Johnsons and their father's first name was Major, too. We never knew my grandmother's husbands. When I was born, she was already a widow.

My grandmother, whom we called Ma'am Ma, was an extremely bright woman who found many ways to augment her meager income. She sometimes planted and harvested small crops for White families who didn't want to be bothered with the responsibility but wanted the food the work produced. Sometimes, White farmers hired her to shell bushels of peas and beans for them. She summoned all of us and we would gather on her front porch, each of us with a pail to capture the peas we shelled. It took hours, but she never let us leave until all the peas or beans had been shelled.

Despite her small frame, Ma'am Ma never seemed to tire. She washed and ironed clothes for White families. Often, her living room would be full of bundles of clothes she had washed and starched and prepared to be ironed. She sewed quilts that she sold to families needing cover for the winter.

She was an entrepreneur, too. During the summer, every Black church had a revival that offered those who were not Christians an opportunity to become one. Each of those intense religious gatherings lasted for two weeks. On the Sunday following the two weeks, those who had joined were baptized and welcomed into the church. It was a festive occasion that lasted all day and drew people from around the parish. Food was prepared and served. But Ma'am Ma saw an opportunity to make a little money. She secured sweets and other confectionery items from the vendor who serviced the corner store near her and set up a tent. It was like having a portable store on the church lawn. Throughout the summer on Sundays, when the various churches in the area celebrated the end of their revival, she operated her little "business." She did well, too.

If a plot of land wasn't being utilized, our grandmother would not rest until she had either rented it or bartered for its use. She had the land plowed and then planted corn, beans, collard greens, and other vegetables that often helped to feed us and others in the community.

She bought PG and me our first baseball shoes. She helped to purchase my first baseball glove and PG's first catcher's mitt. When we needed spending money for school activities, we went to her. Some folks said she was so smart she could have been a schoolteacher when she was younger.

All of Ma'am Ma's sons fought in World War II except her youngest, who was not old enough to go. Uncle Jack, her oldest son, moved to Florida when he returned, so we never knew him. Uncle Fred, the brother born after my father, made a career in the Navy and we saw him only a few times when he came home on leave. Eloise, my father's only sister, lived in Mansfield, mostly with Ma'am Ma. We saw her often. We also saw TJ, the youngest to join the military, at age fifteen, and Sylvester, the baby son, from time to time. Both lived in Shreveport.

Uncle TJ and his wife, Aunt Earline, had four children, three girls and a boy, who spent summers with Ma'am Ma. We had so much fun with them. When summer ended, we were so sad when they had to return home. Sometimes on weekends, Daddy piled all of us in his car and drove to Shreveport to visit them. We were always excited because for us traveling to Shreveport was like going on a vacation.

There was much more to see and to do there than in Mansfield. Cafés and restaurants seemed to be on every street. The downtown streets were broad, unlike most of the narrow streets in Mansfield. Toy stores had different gadgets, sports equipment, bikes, and scooters, items that we couldn't find in the few stores in Mansfield. Visiting Uncle TJ was always a special treat.

My father's family was small. Ma'am Ma was born in Bernice, a town about 114 miles northeast of Mansfield. She then moved to Slagle, a small village in Vernon Parish, about 85 miles south of Mansfield. My father was born there. In 1931, the family moved to Mansfield, when my father was about twelve years old. Few of Ma'am Ma's relatives visited her, except her brother Henry, who came to live with her after he had been injured in a train accident. His body was so broken, he was confined to a bed, unable to do for himself. We suspected White folks had caused it, but neither he nor Ma'am Ma talked about it.

My mother's side of the family was huge. Everywhere I went, I would run into a cousin.

"You don't know me? I'm Aunt Nobie's grandson. I'm your third cousin. Boy, ya gettin' tall. Tell Cousin Lurline I said hello."

"You Wade and Lurline's boy, ain't ya? You don't know me, but I'm your fourth cousin."

Even if you wanted to get away, you couldn't.

Madear was born and raised on a sharecropper's farm. Jack Williams, a major White landowner in DeSoto Parish, owned the land. The Joneses, my mother's family, worked his crops and could use a small portion of the land to grow their own. My mother was the fourth oldest, after a sister and two brothers, and ahead of two younger sisters. When they were old enough, they worked the field alongside their father, Theodore, and their mother, Muriel Elizabeth.

Papa, as we called my mother's father, was a tall, slender, but strong man whose skin was chocolate brown. His grandfather, Jack Jones, Sr., who was born in 1835, had moved to

Louisiana from Georgia. Papa's father was Tom Jones, and his mother, who gave birth to him in 1898, was named Julia.

Papa was a hard worker like his father and grandfather. But working hard didn't mean much on those plantation-like farms in the South. The White owners had established a system that made sharecroppers like Papa dependent upon them, no matter how much they harvested.

Muriel Elizabeth—she was called Shug—had light skin and long black hair. It was said that her family, the Campbells, had moved to Mansfield from Alabama. Folks used to say Grandma Shug was part Indian. A lot of Black people, though, claimed Indigenous ancestry rather than admit to having a White one. Having White ancestry usually meant someone's daughter or sister had been forced to have an illicit relationship with a White man in town.

My mother and her siblings rarely went to school. Working the fields to help the family put food on the table mattered more. When they did go, they had to walk for miles to get there. My mother remembered that many times she and her friends were called names and pelted with rocks by White kids as the Whites-only school bus drove past.

When she was fourteen years old, my mother's life changed profoundly. Grandma Shug caught pneumonia. When she was finally taken to a hospital in Shreveport, nearly forty miles away, it was too late to save her. After her death, in many ways Madear became the mother of the family. The oldest daughter, Aunt Ola Mae, had married and moved a distance away. So preparing meals, washing clothes, and caring for her two younger sisters, Essie and Margaret, became my mother's responsibility. When my mother was seventeen, she gave birth to Mary Jurdine, my older sister. Now she had three youngsters to take care of. Uncle Buddy and Uncle Bruce, her older brothers, depended on her, too. Madear became the family matriarch while she was still just a teenager. It would be her role for the rest of her life, and even extend to include those who were not part of her own biological family.

All Madear's siblings lived in or around Mansfield except Uncle Buddy, who moved to Houston, Texas, to find work. Aunt Essie, the oldest surviving sister after Aunt Ola Mae died when she was thirty-five, lived not far from us. Aunt Margaret lived with us from time to time, and Uncle Bruce had a place in the "country" near our family church. Uncle Buddy had three children; Aunt Essie had two; Aunt Margaret, four; Uncle Bruce, one; and Aunt Ola Mae had five. I had first cousins all over the place. Aunt Essie's and Aunt Margaret's children, the Joneses and the Campbells, made frequent visits to our home.

After his children grew up and moved to town, Papa continued to live in the country. On our visits, we loved running in the field where Papa grew watermelons, peas, corn, and collard greens. But we were always anxious to get home before night descended. There was no electricity in Papa's small wooden house, only kerosene lamps for light. No pipes for running water meant that water had to be collected from an outdoor well. Heat came from a fireplace in the living room, where firewood was always neatly stacked.

After Papa married again, he moved to Mansfield, too. He couldn't read or write, but Papa kept up with news and current events by listening to the radio daily. When he visited us, he and I would sit on the porch discussing what he had heard the previous day. I enjoyed those conversations with my grandfather. Sometimes, we would sit for hours just talking.

"Them Russians something else. They just sent that spaceship up in space."

"Yes, sir. Sputnik."

"What's it called again?"

"Sputnik. Sputnik One."

"Yeah, that's what it's called. And they just did that nuclear test. The United States better watch out. Them Russians will overtake us."

"You think the United States should be exploring in space, Papa?"

"No! No! That's God's territory. Nobody should be tryin' to go where God is. That's blasphemy. We ain't God. God ain't meant for us to go where he is."

"You think God is up in the sky, Papa?"

"God is everywhere. God is all over. He ain't in one place."

Madear often brought coffee to her father during his visits.

"Here, Papa, take this cup. It's hot."

Papa loved his coffee. When he visited, Madear sometimes gave him three or four cups of it. She always had a fresh pot ready when he came.

"Thank you, daughter."

Papa would take the hot cup, hold it for a while so it could cool off, then sip from it.

"You know, you got a smart boy here. He keep up with all the news."

"He read everything he can get his hands on, Papa."

"I wish I knowed how to read."

"You still can, Papa," I said excitedly. "You still can. It ain't hard."

"Naw. I'm too old. I'll just listen to the radio. I keep it on all day and git all the news I need."

"But when you can read, you don't have to depend on no-body else," I said.

"Yes, you do," Papa retorted.

He took another sip from the cup and looked up.

"You gotta depend on the people who write and print what ya reading."

He had a point. But I knew Papa wasn't interested in learning how to read, anyway. He thought what he called "schooling" was for children like me. He thought his time to learn had passed by.

"Your birthday coming up soon, ain't it, Brother?" he asked me.

"Yes, sir. On the twenty-third."

"How old you gonna be?"

"Eleven."

"Well, I'll drop by again to bring you something. Eleven? My, my, time sho' go by fast. It seems like yesterday when you was born."

CHAPTER 4

Starting a Family

In 1946, the average cost of a new house was between $5,000 and $6,000. Twenty-one cents could buy a gallon of gasoline. Eggs were sixty-four cents a dozen. A new car could be purchased for $1,120. The United Nations held its first meeting that year. The first Cannes Film Festival took place. Bluesman B.B. King left his home in Indianola, Mississippi, and traveled to Memphis, Tennessee, where he would eventually launch his musical career. Bikinis went on sale for the first time. Tupperware was introduced to consumers. And, in April 1946, Wade Hudson and Lurline Jones got married.

As a young man, my father volunteered to fight in World War II, the war that political leaders said was waged to secure freedom and to end tyranny. From 1941 to 1945, little else but the war was the topic of conversation, including for Black people.They, too, wanted the world to be safe again.

My father served in a segregated military, meaning that most Black soldiers were assigned menial jobs. In previous wars, such as the Revolutionary War, the Civil War, the Spanish-American War, and World War I, thousands of Black soldiers had proved themselves to be fine fighters when allowed to engage in combat. But that didn't matter. Their bravery and ability were still questioned. Only a few were allowed to become officers.

My father was assigned to the quartermaster division. He drove trucks that carried supplies to the troops fighting on the front line. When we were kids, he used to tell us stories about what it was like during his years of military service in Italy, England, and Algeria, in northern Africa.

Getting supplies to the front was extremely challenging, especially at nighttime, when the men drove their trucks without using headlights. If they were seen, they could be attacked by enemy planes.

"If we didn't get those supplies to the front line, our soldiers wouldn't be able to fight," Daddy would say proudly.

Sometimes, he told us, they had to drive over mountain roads with very little margin for error.

"Every once in a while, we lost someone. But those Colored boys who drove those trucks knew what to do."

"You weren't scared, Daddy?" one of us would ask.

"No, sir. We didn't have time to be scared. We had a job to do."

Our father also told us about the discrimination and prejudice he faced, about being called "n——," "coon," and "monkey" by White soldiers.

"Didn't you say something?! Didn't you fight back?" we

asked, expecting a positive answer. "They couldn't treat you in England and Italy the way they do in Mansfield, could they?"

"Yeah, but we fought back. We spoke up. Sometimes we knocked the hell out of 'em. But they would throw us in the brig, you know, the army jail. Or they would take our stripes away and demote us. So many of the boys I knew lost stripes because they punched out a White boy who called them a bad name."

To further demean and humiliate Black soldiers, my father said, White soldiers would tell Frenchmen, Englishmen, and Italians that Black soldiers had tails.

"Some of them kids hadn't seen Negroes before, so they believed the lies. They would run up to one of us and ask to see his tail, and the White soldiers would fall over laughing."

Tears welled up in my father's eyes as he recounted the painful stories that remained so vivid to him.

The Allied forces, which is what the United States and its partner countries were called, eventually defeated the Axis alliance of Germany, Italy, and Japan and saved the world from their aggression. When my father came back home, he must have felt like those enslaved African Americans who were freed following the Civil War. The freedom they had expected was ultimately denied. My father had risked his life for democracy, but, for him, freedom remained just a stale hope, a wishful thought, an unfulfilled dream. He settled in Mansfield, and in 1946, he married my mother. He was twenty-seven years old.

With money he had saved while in the army, my father

purchased a three-room house on Mary Street for his new family, which included my mother's five-year-old daughter, Mary Jurdine. People called houses like the one he bought "shotgun houses." Many homes in the South during that time began as shotgun houses because they were easier to build and made maximum use of the land the homeowners had acquired. The rooms were lined up one behind the other, typically a living room first, then one or two bedrooms, and finally a kitchen in the back. The joke was that one could fire a bullet through the front door and it would go right out the back door without hitting a wall, so that's why they were called shotgun houses, people said. But "shotgun" also could have been a corruption of the West African word *shogun,* which means "God's house."

As the family grew, my parents added three bedrooms to their house. They had to if they wanted to accommodate the children that seemed to come along every other year.

On October 23, 1946, an eight-pound, bouncing baby boy was born to the happy couple. They named him Wade Hudson Jr., after his father. About a year later, a second son, Willis Fred, was born. Another son died at birth. A fourth son, Wilbert Charles, was born the next year, followed three years later by Curtis Lee. Lauriece, a sister, was next, then Raymond, and finally, Major (Babebro). By the end of the fifties, my mother and father had almost enough children to field their own baseball team, eight in all.

CHAPTER 5

Mischief

The 1950s began with a polio epidemic that primarily affected children. Although it was not widespread, its impact—leaving children in wheelchairs, with leg braces, on crutches, and with deformed limbs—terrified families. Many parents kept their children close to home. There was also the fear of a nuclear attack by the Union of Soviet Socialist Republics. The United States and the USSR were stockpiling atomic weapons that could devastate cities and towns if dropped. To prepare in the United States, air raid and "duck and cover" drills became routine at most schools. The possibility of a nuclear war was a major topic for adults. But I was too young to understand all that. And I was having fun exploring my environment, discovering new things. There was little room for the concerns that occupied adults' time.

By the time I was five years old, there were four children. The three rooms that were added served as bedrooms for the family. The first was my father and mother's. The two remaining rooms were for the kids. Each held beds that we shared and a chest of drawers that often got in the way when we moved around in the rooms. PG and I shared a room. Jurdine and Lillo had the other room.

Our house, as with most houses in our community, had no central heating. A gas heater in the living room provided heat for the house. Cold days during the winter didn't last long. When they came, we used blankets and quilts to keep warm while we slept. On those cold days, we gathered in the living room to be near the heat, only going to our bedrooms to sleep.

Summer days were extremely hot. Temperatures often reached the nineties as the blistering sun beamed down with a vengeance. Electric fans offered a little respite for adults. We children, however, wore shorts and T-shirts, but sometimes the boys wore no shirts at all. We often went barefoot, refusing to let the heat stop us from having fun.

PG and I were always together. Daddy and Madear couldn't afford to buy us the toys we wanted. Those they did purchase usually didn't last very long because they were inexpensive and poorly made. So, even at ages three, four, and five, PG and I depended upon our imaginations to create our own toys. From large rubber bands we made slingshots. We rolled discarded car tires around the yard and up and down the street for fun. I wrapped old cloth around small stones and sewed the cloth tightly to make our own baseballs. Sometimes, we used dried corncob pieces as baseballs and old broomsticks for bats. Instead of miniature cars, we painted small bricks that we found and pushed them across the yard, making the sounds that real cars made. Their not being actual toy cars didn't dampen our excitement. I pretended to be my father driving his old Ford, and PG was Uncle TJ in his Chevrolet.

I was high-spirited, always looking for some new adventure or unfamiliar terrain to explore. Most homes had gas stoves in their kitchens and gas heaters that provided heat for the other rooms. Folks always kept matches handy to light them.

"Brother, go ask Ella for some matches," I heard Madear call to me one day. "We ran out."

"You gonna light the stove?" I asked.

"Yeah. Go get a few from Ella."

I had watched Madear use matches to light the oven many times. She would turn the knob on top of the stove, then bend down to apply the lighted match to the oven below. Magically, fire appeared. So, I knew I could do it, too. I would surprise her and light the oven myself. I ran into the kitchen, turned the gas on, and rushed over to Miss Ella's house.

"Miss Ella, Madear needs some matches," I told our neighbor excitedly. "She told me to see if you got any."

"Here," Miss Ella said, placing a few matches in my hand.

I rushed off.

"What do you say?" she yelled at me.

I stopped.

"Oh, I forgot. Thank you, Miss Ella."

"And stop running! You gonna fall down and hurt yourself."

"Yes, ma'am."

I slowed down, but as soon as I landed on the last step leading from Miss Ella's house, I took off again. After arriving in the kitchen, I bent to my knees, lit a match, and extended it toward the oven. That's all I remember.

"Lord have mercy! Look at this boy's face!" It was Madear, staring at me but keeping her distance.

I heard her scream. As I lay on my back in front of the stove, I felt a pain that was completely foreign to me, and it was coming from my face.

"Brother. Brother, you all right? You all right?"

The voice sounded like Cousin Boot, another one of my mother's cousins. Apparently she had stopped by for her regular afternoon visit, and in my rush to light the oven I had not seen her.

Cousin Boot leaned over me, examining my face.

"We better get him to the hospital, Lurline!"

I was rushed to the hospital in downtown Mansfield.

"He was very lucky," the doctor told my mother. "It could have been much worse. It's only a first-degree burn."

Dr. Grindle was one of several White doctors in Mansfield. There were no Black doctors.

"It'll be sore for a while, but I don't think there'll be any permanent damage."

"You sure, Dr. Grindle? His face won't be scarred, will it?"

"It's burning! It's hurting!" I complained as I sat on the table. I moved my hand toward my face.

"Don't touch it!" Dr. Grindle grabbed my hand and slapped it lightly.

"Make sure he doesn't touch it," he told my mother. "It will certainly get much worse if he does. I'm going to give him some medicine for the pain. In a little while, it won't hurt so much. I'm also going to give you some cream. Put it on his face very gently and follow the directions on the tube. Bring him to my office in a week."

"In a week?"

"Yes, next Wednesday. Call my office to make an appointment."

"Thank you, doctor," my mother responded, somewhat relieved. "I sho' thank you."

Then he asked her, "Why did you let him light that stove, auntie?"

"I didn't let him do that, doctor. That boy is into everything," Madear replied.

Trying to light an oven wasn't my only adventure. Although Daddy loved planting fruit trees, he wasn't very successful at growing them. Once he planted several apple trees that grew but didn't really produce apples. He tried his hand at growing a persimmon tree, but that didn't pan out, either. He found his green thumb, though, when he planted grapevines at the far end of the yard in back of our house. He watered the vines generously and removed weeds and grass that threatened their growth. He built wooden frames to support the fast-growing vines, and every evening after he returned home from a long day at work, he went to check on his grapes. It took a while, but finally, vines bearing sweet, juicy Concord grapes grew in abundance.

Daddy was so happy. He erected a wire fence around the vines to protect them. But that couldn't keep his oldest son from finding his way underneath and into the vines of delicious grapes. Once there, I ate and ate and ate, swallowing seeds and all. After resting for a while, I ate some more. Finally, tired of eating, I lay on my back, so full of delicious grapes, I could barely move.

From a distance I could hear Madear calling.

"Brother! Brother! Where you at, boy?"

But I couldn't respond. I tried to answer but nothing came out, only half-eaten grapes that oozed from my mouth and down my cheek. So, I just lay there, looking up at the clouds that floated above.

When Madear found me, she must have thought I had died and gone to grape heaven.

"Oh, Lord! This boy done got into Wade's grapes."

Again, Cousin Boot was visiting. When she tried to move me, I came alive again and started groaning.

"Look at that boy's stomach," she said, almost laughing. "He look like he pregnant. Look at those vines. See how many grapes are gone."

"Lord, he ate that many grapes?" Madear was aghast when she saw how many were missing from the vines.

"He sho' did," Cousin Boot answered. "Ain't nobody out here but him. We better take him to the hospital. They probably need to pump his stomach."

That's what Dr. Grindle did when Madear took me to the hospital downtown.

"It's you again, auntie?" he told my mother when he came into the Colored waiting room where we were.

"And it's the same boy, again, huh?"

"Yes, sir, he's my oldest son."

I overheard Daddy and Madear arguing about the grapevines when Daddy came to visit me in the hospital after his workday ended.

"You shouldn't of planted them grapes, Wade."

"Lurline, how would I know that boy was gonna try to eat 'em all up?"

"You know he git into everything."

"I put a fence round 'em."

"I could of told ya that wasn't gonna keep him out. That boy always find a way to git into stuff he shouldn't."

"Lurline, growing them grapes gave me something to do, something I could get my teeth into."

Several days later, after I had recovered, I went into the backyard to look at the grapes that had KO'd me. They were not there. Daddy had cut down the vines.

For weeks afterward, he wandered around in the area where he had planted, nurtured, and successfully grown the grapes that had brought him so much pride. Sometimes, I stood on the back porch and watched him just stare at the vacant spot that had once held his grapevines. He had succeeded at something, and it, too, had been snatched away.

My risky behavior continued to get me into trouble.

Daddy built a utility shed in the backyard. There, he kept bushels of sweet potatoes and white potatoes that he stored under straw. He used it to hang slabs of pork that he cured, a process to preserve it. The shed also served as storage for garden tools and for other gadgets our father used around the house. Flour and cornmeal in ten-pound containers were also placed in one corner. Those times when it wasn't padlocked, PG and I would make our way inside, exploring and looking to find something that would pique our interest. One day, we found it. On a narrow shelf in a corner, we spotted a small can. I quickly unscrewed the cap. Inside, we saw white granules that, to me, looked like rice.

But why was rice in a can inside the utility house? I turned to my brother.

"This is rice," I told him. "See?"

PG looked inside the can.

"Taste it," I told him. "It's rice."

I shook a few of the granules from the can into my brother's small hand.

"Go ahead and taste it," I ordered him.

PG put a few of the granules into his mouth. He started screaming and ran from the shed and into the kitchen. Madear was there getting ready to cook dinner.

I wondered what was wrong with my little brother. Why was he running? The rice tasted that bad?

"Brother, come here!" Madear called. "Come here, right now!"

From the tone of her voice, I knew I was in trouble. Again. So I put on my sad, innocent face.

"You called me, Madear?" I asked, after I reached the kitchen. I hoped my blameless demeanor would work.

"What did you give your brother?"

"I just gave him some rice. It was rice."

"Rice? Ain't no rice out there. The only rice in this house is in the cabinet in this kitchen."

"It was rice, Madear. Rice in a can. Somebody put it out there."

"Go get it and bring it here. PG mouth is burning like crazy. It can't be no rice."

I looked at my brother as tears streamed down his face.

"It's still burning! It's burning!"

"Go get what you gave him, I told you! Go get it so I can see what it is!"

I ran to the shed, grabbed the can, and rushed back into the kitchen. She looked at it.

"Boy, this is lye! This ain't no rice! You gonna get it!" Madear said, pointing a finger at me.

I did get it. She broke a switch from the large hedge bush she had planted in our yard and called me into the house.

"Why did you give your brother that lye? Don't you know that lye could of injured him bad?"

"I thought it was rice, Madear! I—I—I really did."

"Why didn't *you* eat it?"

"I thought PG wanted some."

"Well, you're gonna get it."

Madear grabbed me by the arm and gave me a whipping

with the large switch she held. It wasn't the only one I received from her.

Daddy didn't use a switch. When he punished us, he usually did so with his belt.

Madear said little when she delivered her whippings. But Daddy talked and whipped. He would grab us by an arm with his left hand to secure us. And with each lash of the belt, he preached to us.

"Didn't I tell you not to do that?!" A quick whip of the belt followed.

"You gonna listen to me next time?!" Another quick whip of the belt.

"Next time I tell you to do something, you better do it!"

We always wondered what was worse, the whipping or the lecture that came with it.

CHAPTER 6

Preschool at Miss Lizzie B's

When I neared age five, Daddy and Madear sent me to pre-school. Miss Lizzie B, our next-door neighbor and a former elementary schoolteacher, had opened a school in her mother's house to teach children before they entered public school. The public school in Mansfield didn't have kindergarten then. There were six of us in the class. So each of us received Miss Lizzie B's special attention.

I loved preschool. I couldn't wait until the next school day. We sang songs I had never heard before. Miss Lizzie B read stories to us. She loved the Brothers Grimm fairy tales. She also read Joel Chandler Harris's Brer Rabbit stories. "Tar Baby" was one of her favorites. We couldn't get enough, and when she finished reading one story, we demanded another. Miss Lizzie B taught us the letters of the alphabet and how to count. We learned different shapes and colors. She gave us assignments to take home and bring back the next day.

At Miss Lizzie B's, I began to learn what being responsible and respectful meant. Madear and Daddy talked about exhibiting good character a lot. But they seemed to always be fussing when they did it. Miss Lizzie B was not accusatory and seemed to understand that we all mess up sometimes. She was understanding, encouraging, inspiring.

"Brother"—that's what she called me—"you have two younger brothers who look up to you. You have to be a good example to them. If they see you do something, they will do it. Because you're the oldest boy, you have to think not just about yourself, but about them, too."

So I tried hard to not do the shenanigans I had done before.

Once, I overheard Miss Lizzie B tell my mother she thought I was smart and inquisitive. I was "a quick learner," she said. I liked that.

Later, Miss Lizzie B moved away. I wondered where she had gone. No one around us said a word about her departure. A few months later she returned with a baby son she had named Roland.

We never knew who Roland's father was. People speculated that he was a married man. Miss Lizzie B's relationship with him, people whispered, was why she had lost her job as a schoolteacher. During those days, schoolteachers, especially women, had to be beyond reproach.

Miss Lizzie B's mother was a stern, often mean woman who frightened kids in the neighborhood. People stayed away from her. Adults, too. At her insistence, we called her Grandma Lela. She must have been in her seventies when we were youngsters. She always wore an apron and wrapped her head in a scarf. When people neared her house, they tiptoed by. She was that intimidating.

But Grandma Lela respected my father and mother, at least most times. Madear always inquired about her health and offered help if she needed it. If there was minor work to be done around her house, my father volunteered to do it. She would often ask one of us to go to the store for her, always to purchase Dr Pepper soda or rubbing alcohol. Sometimes when we played ball in our yard, an errant throw would land in hers. When she was in a good mood, she threw the ball back to us. When her mood was foul, she would keep it for days. Then, several days later, when we went out to play, we would find the ball in the middle of our yard. She had finally thrown it back.

The first time I heard the word "hoodoo" it was in reference to Grandma Lela. I saw Madear, Aunt Essie, and Cousin Ella Mae looking out the front-room window, watching Grandma Lela bending over near her front porch with a small container in her hand.

"She's putting hoodoo dust down," Aunt Essie said, trying to get a better view.

"Lord, what she up to now?" Cousin Ella Mae wondered.

"Lurline, you better watch your kids. She'll put that hoodoo on them," Aunt Essie warned.

"What's hoodoo?" I asked innocently, looking from Aunt Essie to Cousin Ella Mae to Madear for the answer.

"That's how you put a spell on somebody," Aunt Essie

blurted out, half laughing and half serious. "It's how you get 'em to do what you want 'em to do."

My mother stepped in. "Don't pay Essie no mind, Brother. She don't know what she talkin' 'bout."

"Lurline, you ain't scared to let Brother go over there for school?" Aunt Essie said, still teasing, as she usually did.

"She ain't gonna bother Brother," Madear declared. "She better not. Besides, Lizzie B don't believe in that stuff. She's educated."

After hearing all that talk about hoodoo, I was becoming afraid myself.

Grandma Lela always thought people were trying to harm her, to put a fix on her.

"Lurline, I tell you, I saw 'em throw that bag in my yard and run like the devil. They got something on it. I been scared to come out my house."

"Nobody would do that, Miss Lela. You think so?"

"Lurline, I know so! I've had a headache ever since."

"Lord, Miss Lela, why would anybody wanna do that to you?"

"Just mean and evil, that's all. Just mean and evil. But I got something to fix 'em."

She pointed to a small piece of garlic she had run a string through and placed around her neck.

"Lord, Miss Lela. That's garlic, huh?" Madear said, trying to keep from laughing. "It's sho' strong."

"This will fix 'em," Grandma Lela said proudly. "See, my headache almost gone now. This garlic work every time."

People thought Grandma Lela was weird. But to her, the battle against hoodoo fixes and curses was serious.

I used to wonder how Miss Lizzie B could be Grandma Lela's daughter. They were so different. Miss Lizzie B kept her mother away from her students. Sometimes, however, when we were in class, we could see Grandma Lela standing off at a distance, staring at us. She never bothered us during our school day.

Preschool at Miss Lizzie B's gave me a head start. When I enrolled in first grade at DeSoto Parish Training School, I found out just how much.

CHAPTER 7

Hello, DeSoto Parish Training School

My sister Jurdine attended DeSoto Parish Training School. During previous school years, I had watched every morning as students passed our house carrying their books and school supplies. I saw them return in the afternoon, chatting and playing with each other. What went on at school, I wondered. How different was it from school at Miss Lizzie B's?

These questions and more were on my mind the morning my mother prepared me for my first school day. I wore a new pair of blue jeans, a new shirt, and a new pair of shoes. The day before, my mother had even taken me to get a haircut at Mr. Jefferson's barbershop. I was ready.

"Who's gonna be my teacher?" I asked Jurdine. She was wearing her first-day-of-school clothes, too.

"You won't know until they tell ya," my older sister replied.

"Who was your teacher the first time you went to school?" I continued with my questioning.

"Miss Williams. She's a good teacher."

Soon, my mother, Jurdine, and I started the half-mile walk to school. There was no bus. All of us who lived in town had to walk to school. There were yellow buses to drive students who lived in what we called "the country," where their families lived and worked on farms. Some of them had to rise as early as six o'clock in the morning so they could make the long walk to meet the bus.

The beginning of a new school year was always exciting and special. Not just for students, but for their mothers and fathers, too. Parents in Mansfield placed a lot of faith in the teachers' ability to provide a high-quality education for their children. Most of them saw education as a chance for their children to have a better life. That's why DeSoto Parish Training School was established.

It began as the Mansfield Colored School in 1913, when two teachers taught in a two-room building. In 1915, educator Dewitt Johnson was brought to Mansfield to head the school. "Professor Johnson," as he was affectionately called by Black people in Mansfield, was a visionary in the tradition of Booker T. Washington and Mary McLeod Bethune, who founded Black schools in the South.

"Four acres of land and a two-room school, granted for a three-month period with an attendance of less than fifty pupils was the story of public education for Blacks in Mansfield prior to 1915," wrote Professor Johnson about the challenge he and his wife, Elizabeth, faced that first year.

The professor moved quickly. With the help of Elizabeth,

he began building a school that would attract Black students from around DeSoto Parish. At first, for additional classroom space, he rented rooms in houses near the school. Later, he organized community groups to help raise money to build more classrooms and to help purchase school supplies and materials. He constantly urged a reluctant and sometimes resentful White school board to provide more funds than the meager amount they usually allocated. He borrowed money himself when they said no. He secured support for the Rosenwald Fund, established to help underfunded Black schools in the South. In 1928, the DeSoto Parish Training School held its first graduating ceremony for twelve students.

Madear and I made our way into a long green building that had been freshly painted. Outdoor restrooms, one for boys and one for girls, were at the end of the building. For most of us, outdoor toilets weren't unusual. They were quite common in rural areas and in small towns where there was no municipal sewage system.

Inside the classroom, Miss Lula Williams, a heavyset, matronly woman, met Madear and me. Other parents and their children had already made their way inside.

"Good morning, Mrs. Hudson," she said, greeting Madear.

"Mornin', Miss Williams. Good to see you again," Madear responded. "This is Wade Jr., Miss Williams. I know you'll do a good job with him."

"Yes, we will," Miss Williams assured my mother. "You can have a seat, young man."

I looked around the large room filled with desks. At Miss Lizzie B's, we hadn't had desks. We sat on the living room floor. I looked at the large green board attached to the wall behind a much larger desk I assumed was for the teacher. Miss Lizzie B had a portable board and no desk.

Soon, Madear and all the other parents left. I felt a little sad without my mother. I had been with her every day for five years. She was always there, watching us, trying to keep me out of mischief, encouraging me. Even when I attended pre-school at Miss Lizzie B's, she was only a few yards away. Now I would have to go all day without seeing her, and without seeing PG and Lillo.

Miss Williams closed the door to the classroom and my first day at DeSoto Parish Training School began.

I had never been in one room with so many boys and girls my age before. They were tall and dark-skinned, short and light-skinned; they had curly hair and kinky hair, broad lips and large noses, thin lips and small noses. They came from different areas of Mansfield. Most of them I hadn't seen before. Now they were my classmates.

I sat at a desk in the center of the room and kept my eyes on Miss Williams.

"I want each of you to introduce yourself. Stand and tell us your name," she said.

The eager but nervous students looked at each other. Then, Miss Williams pointed to the left side of the room and directed the first student to stand before speaking.

"Go ahead, young man."

"Johnnie Lee Blow."

"Earnie Marie Washington."

"Frank Pea."

"Lois Woodley is my name."

"Ethel Lucille Talbert."

"David Jones."

"Dicie McCoy."

"Maxie Ray Bradford."

"Wanda Faye Hudson."

Finally, it was my turn.

"Wade Hudson," I announced.

"Wade Hudson Jr.," Miss Williams corrected.

I didn't say anything.

"You are a junior, aren't you? That's what Mrs. Hudson said."

"Yes, ma'am," I relented, and sat back down.

Why did she have to insist on calling me Wade Hudson Jr.? I thought. I didn't like being called Junior. *It's a wonder Madear didn't say "This is Brother,"* the name I was called at home.

The first few days at DeSoto Parish Training School went smoothly, except for Miss Williams calling me Wade Jr.

But the excitement of my first week ended when I was jumped by two classmates, the twins Floyd and Lloyd Jones, during morning recess. We were at play in the schoolyard.

"I had it first," Lloyd insisted, trying to grab the ball I had brought with me from the classroom.

"No, you didn't. I brought it with me!" I argued.

"I don't care. Give it here."

Lloyd reached for the ball, but I moved it away. He pushed me and I dropped the ball and tackled him to the ground.

"Leave me alone. Get off me," he yelled.

Suddenly, I felt a sharp pain on the back of my head. I turned and saw Floyd running away. Lloyd scrambled to his feet and ran off, too.

"You bleeding!" one of my classmates told me excitedly. "You bleeding!" she repeated for emphasis.

Other classmates gathered around, pointing at me.

"I'm going to get Miss Williams," one of them said, and rushed off to where the teacher stood.

"Miss Williams! Miss Williams! One of them twins hit Wade with that soda bottle. They some bad boys. Both of 'em ran away."

Miss Williams escorted me to the classroom and cleaned up the blood as best she could. She sent for Jurdine and told her what had happened.

"It's just a superficial cut," she told my sister. "But I think you should take him home."

To say Madear was angry was a major understatement.

"What did those bad boys do to my son?!" she asked angrily.

Daddy was upset, too. Madear went to the school the next day to voice her concern to Miss Williams.

"Mrs. Hudson, I am so sorry this happened. But I assure you it won't happen again. We have already disciplined the twins."

"But why did they hit my son with a bottle? They could of hurt him really bad."

"You're right, Mrs. Hudson. It could have been much worse. But the twins have apologized. You know, all of our students have a lot to learn."

"Me and my husband try to teach our children to treat people right, Miss Williams. Brother wouldn't never hit another child with a bottle. He know it ain't right."

"The twins know it isn't right now, too, Mrs. Hudson. Please believe me that we will make sure nothing like this ever happens again. Not just to your son but to anyone's child."

The talk with Miss Williams helped Madear calm down. But not Jurdine. The next day, my big sister went to school ready for war. I was still at home healing, but I heard what happened.

My sister cornered the twins.

"Why you hit my brother with that bottle?" she asked them. "I don't know which one of you did it, 'cause I can't tell you apart. Y'all look just alike. But one of you did it."

The twins' older brother and sister, closer to Jurdine's age, came to their siblings' rescue. I got word that my big sister whipped all four of them. A teacher had had to come to their aid.

My first months as a first grader were really a replay of what I had learned at Miss Lizzie B's. Not only could I count by single numbers already, but I could also do so by fives and tens. I knew the letters of the alphabet, basic shapes and colors, and all the other concepts Miss Lizzie B had taught so well. I was a good reader for a five-year-old, too. I had already read many of the stories Miss Williams read to the class. I knew what was going to happen in "Jack and the Beanstalk" and "Hansel and Gretel." When Miss Williams asked the class a question, I usually knew the answer and shouted it out to her. Finally, she insisted that I stop because it was unfair to the other students. So, the first half of the school year was boring for me. When Miss Williams introduced things I hadn't been taught at Miss Lizzie B's, my interest was sparked.

In school, I discovered girls. Or, rather, I discovered Wanda Faye Hudson. I had a crush on her that lasted throughout elementary school. Although we had the same last name, we were not related.

Wanda Faye was always my first order of business when I arrived in class in the morning. I checked to see if she was there. She rarely missed a day. But those few days she did miss were downers for me. I wanted to go home, too. If Wanda Faye wasn't at school, I didn't want to be there, either.

Tall and slender, Wanda Faye was a better dresser than the other girls. Her hair was always neatly styled. She had class, even if she was only six or seven years old. One day she was going to be my wife, I resolved.

Wanda Faye lived on Gibbs Street near Louise Street, about a mile from where I lived. The grocery store where my family shopped was down the street from her house. Whenever Daddy and Madear went food shopping, I jumped into the car, hoping to see Wanda Faye when the car passed her house. Sometimes I did see her sitting on her front porch, reading a book. I'd wave and she would wave back. My day was made.

With each passing school term, I became even more interested in Wanda. I sat on the steps often, daydreaming about her. I lay awake at night thinking about her. I didn't even mind her being ahead of me in class ranking.

Every year, the school held fundraisers called a "drive." The classes competed to see who could raise the most money. Parents baked cookies and made sandwiches to sell. Teachers purchased candy bars in bulk and sold them to students. The drive, which lasted for weeks, was a major activity at school. The money we earned was used to purchase much-needed school supplies and to support athletic programs. It was what our parents and teachers always had to do—find ways to make something out of a little.

At the end of the drive, each class chose a king and queen, the students who had raised the most money.

One year, Wanda Faye asked me to help her campaign to be queen.

"You want *me* to help *you*?" I asked.

"Yeah. You can help me sell the candy bars I just got. I can't win by myself."

I sold a lot of candy bars that school year. I even brought some home and sold them. Wanda Faye won. She beamed when our third-grade teacher, Miss Hill, announced that she was queen for the year. I beamed, too.

Unfortunately, my crush remained my very own secret. I was too shy to even explore the possibility of Wanda Faye being "my girlfriend." After she moved away during the ninth grade, I never saw her again.

I liked going to school. I liked playing football and baseball with the Mary Street Boys and hanging out with the other kids in the neighborhood. But I liked family gatherings just as much. They were always special times, especially Christmas, the biggest holiday in Black Mansfield.

Every year, families began preparing months in advance so that the Christmas holiday would be just as memorable as the previous one. Many parents put their children's toys on layaway early in the year because they knew they wouldn't be able to buy them with one payment.

I loved the Christmas spirit. I loved the Christmas dinners, the community fellowship, and the Christmas-love people shared. We decorated the tree enthusiastically and waited impatiently for Christmas Day so we could see what Santa had brought us.

Madear usually started buying and stockpiling ingredients she needed to cook the Christmas dinner in early December. Then, two or three days before Christmas, she began cooking. We often helped by peeling both white and sweet potatoes, beating egg whites for meringue, and running to the store to get items Madear had forgotten to purchase or had run out of. The kitchen was my mother's domain for those pre-Christmas days. Several turkeys were roasted. Corn bread dressing, potato salad, and collard greens were prepared, as well as a variety of desserts, including sweet potato, peach, and egg pies and pineapple, chocolate, and lemon cakes. Some Christmases, Madear would add her famous fruitcake to the offering.

On Christmas Eve, we were so excited we couldn't fall asleep.

"Go to sleep, or Santa will pass us by," my father warned.

I closed my eyes and waited for sleep to come.

On Christmas morning, PG and I rose early. We sneaked slowly into the living room to peek underneath the Christmas tree. Had Santa passed us by? The toys our father and mother had asked Santa to bring were never what we wished for, the ones that sent our imaginations soaring when we saw them in the Sears Roebuck catalogs. We were still happy that Santa had come, though. A few hours later, as we played with our new toys, the day perked up for adults, too, as they began to embrace that special holiday. As they walked past our house, folks yelled greetings from the street.

"Merry Christmas, y'all!"

"Merry Christmas," we yelled back.

"Where my Christmas gift?"

"Santa forgot and took it back with 'im!"

"Oh, he passed me by this time, huh? Merry Christmas, anyway. I'll get that gift next Christmas."

Some stopped by for a plate of food, unembarrassed to make special requests known.

"I want some of that turkey, a little of that dressing, potato salad, and a big slice of that pineapple cake and that potato pie. Leen, you sho' can cook!"

Madear always honored the requests and the visitors left with a paper plate piled high with food. It would be that way for days, people dropping by for a holiday meal, until New Year's Day came and went or until Madear ran out of food. The expenses required for this festive celebration always placed a burden on my mother and father. Bills that were due during the coming months were often paid late as they struggled to recover and get back on their feet.

"Y'all happy?" Daddy would ask at the end of Christmas Day, smiling as if he knew the answer to come.

"Yeah!" we replied.

"I'm glad," he would tell us, still smiling, even as he prepared for another long workday.

During the summer, the kids who lived on Mary Street picked wild blackberries and plums. Late afternoons, when the sun eased up, we all played hide-and-seek and other games, racing each other, falling, skinning knees and bruising elbows. Twenty or more of us, boys and girls, cousins and friends, often played together, laughing, singing, and just being kids.

At night, when it was dark—always when it was dark— Madear sat on the sofa and told ghost stories that scared us to death. She swore they were true. We sat transfixed.

"One night, all the men went to a meeting about a new school. And all the women and children went over to Aunt Nobie's house so we wouldn't be alone with no men around. Y'all know Aunt Nobie, Papa's baby sister.

"Well, I was just a little girl, and Essie and Margaret were little things, too. Bruce and Buddy went with the menfolks.

We all started singing, even us children. We was having a grand ol' time. Then, suddenly, we heard a plate crash to the floor in the kitchen and break into pieces. At first, Mama and them thought one of the chillun had sneaked into the kitchen and dropped it. But all the chilluns was with us. Then another plate hit the floor, and another, and another. It seemed like every dish in the kitchen was breaking.

"'Lord have mercy! What's going on?' Aunt Nobie called out. All of us was scared to death. We was afraid to go outside, 'cause at night it got so dark you couldn't see your hand in front of your face. But we was scared to stay in the house, too. So we all huddled in the corner of the room, just shaking. Then, suddenly, we heard a loud noise that sounded like the wall of the kitchen was being pulled apart. We was terrified! No one said a word. We was afraid that whatever it was would soon come to get us. We stayed huddled together in that corner till the men came.

"'What's wrong with y'all?' they wanted to know when we let them in.

"'Somebody's in the kitchen, breaking everything in sight,' Mama said, still shaking.

"The men went into the kitchen to investigate. Papa came out shaking his head. The floor was covered with broken glass and the cabinet that the dishes had been in had been pulled down to the floor from the wall where it had been nailed.

"Papa said, 'That ain't nobody but Callie!'

"Callie was his and Aunt Nobie's oldest sister, who had

died a little while earlier. He told Aunt Nobie that Aunt Callie came back because Aunt Nobie had done her so bad when she was sick. Papa made Aunt Nobie apologize to Aunt Callie. Then he went back into the kitchen and yelled just as loud as he could.

" 'Callie, you get away from here, you hear! Nobie said she was sorry. You get back now!' "

"Did that really happen, Madear?" we wanted to know.

"I swear it did. You can ask Papa the next time you see him. Ask Aunt Nobie."

"Ain't no such thing as a ghost!" I declared.

"Don't say that, boy," Madear came back at me. "Ask Buddy and Bruce. They'll tell ya."

Madear certainly was convincing, especially with ghost stories and scary tales. We stayed up if we could, too afraid to go to bed, scared Aunt Callie would come to get us, too.

When we asked Aunt Nobie if it was true, she said yes.

On Saturdays, when he didn't have to go to work, Daddy showed me, PG, and the other Mary Street Boys baseball tips.

"When you catch the ball, let it come to you." He would demonstrate, with his right hand pushed awkwardly into a glove meant for a right-hand thrower. Daddy was a lefty.

"Don't push at it," he continued. "Hold your glove this way and just let the ball come to you. Don't fight it. Now, let me see you do it."

After watching the demonstration intently, we would give it a try.

When we had finally gotten it, Daddy would say, "There you go! That's what I'm talkin' 'bout. That's the way the pros do it."

We were happy youngsters, growing up together on Mary Street, on the east side of Black Mansfield. It was our own little world, and we ran in it with glee.

CHAPTER 8

The Other Mansfield

"Brother, you and PG be careful," Madear yelled to us from inside the house as we walked down the front porch steps.

"Y'all stay in your place," she continued. "I don't want y'all to get in no trouble. Trouble so easy to get into."

Madear was now at the front door, and she held it open as she watched my younger brother and me walk out of the yard and into the street. We were going downtown.

"Y'all hear me. Y'all hear what I'm telling you?"

"We hear ya, Madear," I responded. "We know. We know."

And we were beginning to know. As we grew, we learned the things that had to be passed down for our survival.

As we continued to the bus stop, we could see Madear still standing in the doorway. She had allowed us to make the thirty-minute trip to buy shirts with money we had earned from running errands for neighbors. We knew that she was now regretting that she had given us permission to go. So we hurried before she could call us back. Besides, we knew how to conduct ourselves. I was ten and PG was nine. We weren't kids anymore.

But I knew why Madear was worried. She always warned us to stay in our place when we were around White people. She, like all Black people in Mansfield, knew what could happen if we didn't. Years of examples that included brutal beatings, being forced to leave town, and even being murdered were whispered about and passed on to each generation. A Black man had been shot and killed by the White owner of a large business where the Black man worked. The White man loaned his Black worker a small sum of money and deducted a portion from the Black man's salary as repayment. The Black worker missed several weeks of work. The White owner, furious about his unpaid loan, searched for the Black man and cornered him underneath a house in a Black neighborhood.

"Where's my money!" he yelled. "Where's my money!"

Without a second thought, without hesitation, he fired a pistol at the Black man and killed him.

"Drag that n—— from under there," he then told another Black man who was nearby.

Nothing happened to the White man. It was "business as usual."

That's why our mother and father drilled precautions into us over and over, and other Black folks modeled for us what to do and what not to do when we were around White people. But I was an inquisitive young Black boy, always searching for answers and wondering why things couldn't be different.

PG and I hurried to the old pine tree at the corner of Mary

and Willard Streets that served as the official bus stop and waited for the city bus everyone called Nickel Willie. Driven by an older White man, the run-down bus was never on time. Sometimes folks waited for more than an hour for it to appear. It broke down often, too. But it was the only public transportation in Mansfield.

This time, my brother and I didn't have to wait very long. We saw it rambling down Mary Street from several blocks away. When it arrived, the old door struggled to open. We entered and moved to the Black section, in the back. Once we were seated, the old bus rambled onward again, maneuvering its way noisily over the potholes and unpaved streets of the east side.

We smiled as it passed people sitting on their porches, fanning themselves for relief from the heat, some drinking lemonade or a cold soda. A few waved and we waved back.

"Where y'all going on that bus?" someone wanted to know.

"Downtown," I answered.

"Tell Lurline I said hi."

"We will."

"Don't spend all that money."

"We ain't got much."

"You joshing me. Why ya going to town, then?"

These were people I knew. I didn't know all their names, but I knew their faces, their family ties. When I went to the grocery store with my parents, I saw them. I saw them on the street or riding in cars as they passed our house. I saw them on their way to work or when they returned home. And

I saw them when work had worn down their bodies and they had gotten too old to do it anymore. Then they sat on their porches drinking lemonade, coffee, or a cold beer, remembering the old days and watching out for the community. I saw some of them when they drank too much alcohol and fumbled their words out of their mouths when they tried to speak. Sometimes they struggled to keep from falling because the alcohol had overcome them. I heard them curse around children and then wish they could take the bad words back. I heard some of them offer comforting prayers in church and sing songs of praise. I saw them support each other when a crisis came, like when someone's house burned down or when a loved one died. These were the people I knew.

The old bus moved past their houses, down Willard Street, turned left onto Roach, then several blocks later made another left turn onto Gibbs, and continued through the east side headed for Polk, the main street to downtown. Once we reached Polk, we had left familiar neighborhoods and were in the White part of town. The streets were paved and better kept, and the closer we got to downtown the more stylish the houses looked. The White residents owned businesses, taught school, were nurses, or held other professional jobs. Some had inherited their lofty status from grandparents who had profited from slavery. They were unlike the White people who lived in the rural areas. Those working-class and poor Whites had more in common with Black people, but they refused to or simply didn't recognize it.

The once-talkative Black folks on the bus were now quiet.

The unfamiliar territory offered no protection or sense of comfort.

PG and I exited at the part of Polk Street where a small number of department stores and businesses were located.

Most of the buildings in downtown Mansfield had been built decades before, in the 1920s and 1930s and even earlier. A few brick buildings held sway among the wooden ones, most needing new paint jobs, some even facelifts. The entire downtown area could be covered in a ten- to fifteen-minute walk.

While walking the sidewalks, we gave way when a White person approached. No smiling White faces greeted us. We were treated like strangers in our own town, unwanted or at best tolerated. As always, the few Black folks we passed smiled to acknowledge us.

PG and I walked directly to the shirt section of McLaurin's Department Store. Few people were shopping that day. We were the only Blacks there.

PG moved to the other end of the rack that held the shirts. We both were careful not to place any of them too close to our bodies. Again, we had learned well.

"I like this one," I told my brother, holding up a blue short-sleeved shirt. He nodded.

After making our selections, we went to the checkout counter.

"You boys got what you looking for?" the blond, short-haired, middle-aged White salesclerk asked us.

We nodded yes.

"You boys got good taste."

We didn't look directly at her. If you were a Black male, no matter how young, you knew better.

Don't look at a White woman!

Don't look a White man in the eyes.

The clerk folded my shirts first and placed them in a bag. I gave her my money, and she gave me the bag with the shirts in it and my change. Then PG paid for his.

"Y'all seem like nice boys," she continued. "Y'all stay that way. Don't y'all get uppity and big-headed, you hear?"

We didn't say anything as we walked quickly toward the exit. I looked back. The cashier had sat down in a chair behind the counter and was holding a newspaper in her hands.

So far, so good. No trouble.

Because we were thirsty, we found a soda machine and bought Cokes. We never considered finding a "Colored Only" drinking fountain. Our parents always told us we could wait until we got home to get a drink of water.

When we returned home, Madear breathed a sigh of relief.

"What took y'all so long? Y'all had me worried," she told us. "Something told me not to let y'all go."

"That bus is slow, that's all," I said.

But we were home safely! And Madear was all right now.

I tried to understand the intricacies of navigating a racist society. Yes, I had heard how badly Black people were treated in Mississippi and Alabama. I had heard about Money, Mississippi, where a young Black boy named Emmett Till had been killed. I saw the picture of his battered body lying in a coffin, in *Jet* magazine. I knew that Montgomery, Alabama, was a terrible place for Black people to live. I knew about the bus boycott led by Dr. Martin Luther King Jr. *Jet* covered that, too. Many of the awful things that happened to Black people in the South were reported in *Jet* and *Ebony*.

I thought it was all unfair, all the things we couldn't do just because we were "Colored" and the way grown-up Black people had to act like children when they were around White people.

I had to watch my own father defer to White people. I cringed when I saw the pain on his face become more and more evident as White people ordered him around in front of his own sons. It was clear to me that he had little power around these White folks, and that these people were willing to use all their power to exert control over Black people in all situations.

Why? Why is it like this for Black people? I wondered one day after hearing how the police had roughed up a group of Black people waiting to enter the Colored section of the movie theater downtown. Forced to stand in line against a wall so that White theatergoers could go in first, several Black youngsters grew restless and began wandering away from the wall. The White police officers pounced quickly and began shoving and hitting them, injuring some.

"Daddy, why can't we do something about the way White people treat us?!"

"Son," he answered, removing one of the King Edward cigars he usually kept between his lips. Whenever he was about to tell me something important or serious, he called me "son." "It takes all I got to take care of y'all kids and your mother. I gotta put food on the table and keep a roof over your heads. It ain't easy. It ain't easy. The way we treated bothers me, too. But I try to do the best I can for y'all! I gotta take care my family."

Slowly, Daddy turned away. His measured steps told me the question had bothered him. I saw him walk out into the yard. A few minutes later, I heard the engine of his old Ford rev up and he soon drove off, perhaps looking for a place where he could escape racism for just a little while.

Just as it had been during slavery and even afterward, cotton was still king in Mansfield. There was an iron foundry that made metal castings and a company that built trailers for trucks. Domestic work was an industry, too. Black people weren't paid enough to "get by on," as they used to say, so many had to find other ways to augment their meager salaries.

During the week, mornings in our communities were animated with life as people prepared for another workday.

"Morning" was the normal greeting.

"Morning to you" came the response.

"Another good day, huh?"

"Any day that the Lord has made is good."

The replies were always quick and sure.

Melodies filled the air, too. Sometimes it was a blues tune, other times a gospel song. But folks sang, even those who didn't have a voice for it.

During the fall, long before I had risen from my night's sleep, some folks waited patiently for the trucks to take them to pick cotton on the large farms that were reminders of the Southern plantation days. Adults, older folks, and youngsters were there, wearing their assorted hats to protect them from the sun. Some of my schoolmates were among them. They wouldn't attend school until the work on those large "plantations" had been completed. All of the pickers earned three dollars for every one hundred pounds of cotton they picked. They dragged a six-foot-long burlap sack down rows of cotton, picking until it was filled. Some were so good at it, they picked three hundred pounds in a day, which usually lasted until sundown. That's when they called it a day, too, often too exhausted to do anything more than eat a meal, sleep, and get ready for the next workday.

My brothers, sisters, and I never picked cotton. Madear and Daddy didn't allow us to. They had had enough experiences themselves with what Daddy called "that modern form of slavery" to know that fate should not be passed on to their children.

Many of the men in Mansfield were loggers. They cut down trees, trimmed the branches away, and piled them on logging trucks. The trees could be transported to sawmills, where they were turned into lumber, or shipped to paper mills, where they would be converted into paper products. The Wyatt brothers were loggers. I used to watch them come home at the end of the day, dirty and tired. The work was hard and dangerous, but I never heard them complain. It was a job.

Early risers also included Black domestic workers, whom White people called "maids." My mother became one after my brother Major was born. In Mansfield, if you were White, you didn't have to be rich to hire a maid. Many White families could afford to pay the fifteen dollars a week most maids earned. If there was hard work to be done, Black people did it.

At day's end, when the sun had moved westward across the sky and the daily hustle had subsided, few songs filled the air. Steps were slower. Greetings had lost their enthusiasm. Black folks were tired! The day had been long and the work backbreaking. But they would rise the next morning to continue a routine that many had followed most of their lives.

CHAPTER 9

Making the Grades

At the end of each six-week marking period, I rushed home to show my parents my report card. I made the honor roll in every period. By the third grade, I had earned a reputation as a smart student, and that reputation followed me in every school year afterward.

In the third and fourth grades, shooting marbles at school became my favorite hobby. PG and I shot marbles at home in our yard and sometimes with the neighborhood boys. But at school, it was different. Those boys were pros, and some of them were older. We met in the morning to play, about an hour before school started, and sometimes again after school. Usually, a dirt area away from the gaze of teachers was secured. We all brought our stashes of marbles. Some guys had their pockets filled with them. The ones who were good kept their large collections in small cloth bags.

When shooting marbles, you must get down on your knees to knock the marbles from the ring. Every marble shot out of it belonged to the shooter. But getting on your knees often wore out the knees of your pants. Our mothers fussed at us for "destroying" our good school pants. But we kept right on playing. Joe Curtis Pugh, Frank Pea, David Jones, and other boys in my class joined the group every morning, stopping only when the bell rang for school to start. I usually broke even. Some days I won, and I gleefully showed off the highly prized cat's-eye marbles I had netted. Some days I lost, and it ruined my school day as I pouted over my defeat.

By the fifth grade my interest in shooting marbles had waned. Getting to school early now meant playing what we called "cut throw" football. Most of the boys I played with were much bigger than I was. Some were members of a small group of incorrigibles who sometimes terrorized other students. They often hung out in the boys' bathroom, smoking and playing hooky. We weren't allowed to use profanity, but these boys used it as if no other words existed. My parents warned me to stay away from them and not to play with them, but I didn't listen.

"Cut throw" football was just as merciless as it sounds. It really didn't follow any football rules. We boys found pleasure in piling on top of the person who had been tackled. Teammates joined the pile, too. Sometimes twenty to thirty boys piled on top of an unfortunate runner carrying the football. One morning that unfortunate runner was me. When I was tackled, I tried to protect my head by putting my hand between it and the hard ground. I wasn't quick enough. As bodies piled on top, my head was pinned against the ground.

"Get off me!" I yelled. But no one moved.

I could barely breathe. The ordeal seemed to last for an eternity. When the boys finally got up from the pile, I tried to get up, too, but I was so dizzy, I could barely stand. I staggered to a large boulder some yards away, sat down, and braced my back against it. When the bell to start school rang, I tried to get up but couldn't. So I sat and just waited until the dizziness subsided. Finally, I was able to make my way to class. When our teacher asked why I was late, I said I had had to go to the boys' room. Out of the corner of my eye, I could see some of the guys snickering. They knew what had happened.

In the fifth grade, Joseph Glenn joined our class after the school year had already begun.

I don't know why, but I identified with those who were made fun of, laughed at, pointed at, yelled at, just because they happened to be different.

Maybe it was the boy who didn't run the way others thought boys should run, so he was called a "sissy." Maybe it was the girl who dressed shabbily and always looked unkempt and others thought she had less worth than they did. Maybe it was the large girl who had matured faster than the other girls and was ridiculed. Or maybe it was the chubby boy whom the other students called "fat." I related to their pain, their being shunned, being defined and treated like the "other." Maybe it was the way I saw my parents come to the rescue of the vulnerable. Maybe it was the way our church teachings encouraged us to be compassionate and caring. Maybe it was all of that. And maybe it was me, just who I am.

Joseph Glenn was African American with albinism, as was his sister, who was a grade below him. Because their bodies produced little to no melanin, the pigment that provides color, their skin, hair, and eyebrows were white.

Some students were unfriendly to Joseph just because he looked different. Most ignored him. Often, he sat alone, his head lowered, his eyes glued to his desk. Sometimes he would pull out a sheet of paper and begin drawing. As he focused on his work of art, he seemed to be at peace, content.

One day I peeked at one of his drawings.

"What's that?" I asked.

He didn't answer but continued to draw.

"That's a cowboy you drawing, ain't it? That looks like a *real* cowboy."

Joseph smiled. It was the first smile I had seen during the week he had been at school.

"I got a lot more drawings like these," he finally said in almost a whisper. "You wanna see some of them?"

"Yeah! You can really draw. You know, you can sell 'em and make money."

"Naw, I don't wanna sell 'em. I can give you one if you want it."

"How long you been drawing?"

"All my life, I guess. Ever since I can remember."

"Some people say some folks are born with special gifts. Maybe that's you."

"I don't know. Maybe. I just love to draw."

Joseph stood up and his face brightened into a proud smile.

"I sent one of my drawings to a contest in a magazine," he told me.

"Really? Did you win?"

He sat down at his desk again.

"Naw. I didn't win." The smile was now gone.

"Those folks don't know what they doing. I bet your drawing was better than any of 'em."

The following day after school, I heard a knock at our front door. Madear answered it.

"Brother, someone to see you."

It was Joseph Glenn. He had a stack of drawings that he held proudly in his hands. We sat on the sofa and he showed all of them to me.

"You can pick any you want," he offered. "I'll give 'em to you."

I chose three.

Joseph and I became good friends during that year he spent at DeSoto. He visited our house often. Madear and Daddy allowed me to tack the drawings he had given me on our living room wall. His face lit up when he saw them.

Joseph's quietness hid his sense of humor. He was the reason I stopped playing cut throw football. My personal ordeal should have been enough, but it wasn't. One morning, Joseph was the victim.

Occasionally, some of the players on a team tried to block for the runner carrying the ball for them. Some even blocked for me when I was smashed to the ground. They piled on afterward, but they did block. But when they gave Joseph the ball, no one blocked for him. All his teammates stood laughing as the opposing team ganged up on him and threw him violently to the ground. Then they all piled on top of him with knees and elbows first, even his teammates. After pinning him to the ground for a long, excruciating time, they allowed him to get up. They all ran away, laughing and patting each other on the back.

Joseph's nose was bloodied, and his left arm was scratched badly.

"You all right?" I asked.

"Yeah, I'm all right," he mumbled.

"That wasn't right! That wasn't right!"

He looked at me for a long moment but said nothing. The two of us walked to class together. Joseph was too crushed to say anything. Maybe he expected the opposing players to gang up on him. But I think he was surprised that none of his teammates had blocked for him. He knew he had been set up. That was the last time I went to school early to play football.

Joseph and I talked about many things during our times together. I missed him when he didn't return for the next school year.

I didn't always take a stand and reach out to those who

were bullied or shunned because they were different or perceived to be weaker. There were times when I sat by, like most others, not saying anything for fear I would become the target. But my heart ached and my spirit plummeted every time I saw it happen.

CHAPTER 10

TV, Radio, and Rock and Roll

Shake, rattle, and roll!
Shake, rattle, and roll!

While Big Joe Turner's hit song played on radio station KOKA, my sister taught me how to swing, or "swing out," as it was called in Mansfield.

Very few could dance like Jurdine. She would swirl me around, dip to her knees, kick out her right leg, grab me, and spin me around. Before long I was a good dancer, too, moving easily to the music that we listened to on the radio.

The decade of the 1950s was a time of change that set the tone for the 1960s, which were even more dramatic. The fifties were the decade of inventions or popularizations of such now-common things as the credit card, laser, videotape recorder, commercial computer, power steering for cars, and color television. It was the decade of the Korean and Vietnam wars, the beginning of the space race, the *Brown v. Board of Education* Supreme Court decision that declared separate schools for Blacks and Whites unconstitutional, the murder of Emmett Till. And the growth of rock and roll, R & B, and Black radio.

Television was relatively new, and radio stations that had dominated the airwaves for years felt threatened by its growing popularity. National television companies like NBC, CBS, and ABC aggressively added new programs. Radio stations began to change formats to attract new listeners, including Black people. Radio stations that catered to Black communities grew and grew. By 1956, more than four hundred stations across the country played Black music and covered Black news and events.

The first Black radio station near Mansfield was KOKA. Established in Shreveport in 1950, it played R & B and blues, the kinds of music that we heard mostly on jukeboxes and at house parties. KOKA was where I heard all the latest R & B and rock and roll hits released in the 1950s.

Some church folks called it "devil music." But that didn't stop young people like me from listening to the music that made us dance and sing along.

We watched television, too, including shows such as *Captain Kangaroo, The Howdy Doody Show, The Mickey Mouse Club, The Roy Rogers Show,* and *Superman* at Ma'am Ma's house when she purchased the first television set in the neighborhood. When we got a television, I stayed up at night watching late-night movies. Often, while everyone else slept, my eyes were fixed on the television screen until the stations signed off at midnight. Those movies fascinated me with their engaging dialogue, interesting plots, and characters.

Black performers on television were rare. When one did appear, the word got around quickly in the community.

There weren't many Black actors in movies, either. Sidney Poitier, Dorothy Dandridge, Harry Belafonte, Ruby Dee, and Ossie Davis were among the few, but I never got to see them because White theaters in the South wouldn't show their movies.

But Mansfield had its own talent. In churches, powerful voices lifted spiritual messages. Folks learned to play the piano, guitar, and other instruments, and they sang in quartets and choirs.

Aunt Essie had a beautiful voice. When she was younger, she sang in nightclubs before, she said, "turning my life over to the Lord." Her daughters Willie Ruth and Elizabeth Ann could also sing, especially Elizabeth Ann, who had a gifted voice. She came to our house often to sing with Curtis, Lillo, Lauriece, and Raymond. It seemed that half of Mansfield could play the guitar, including Curtis, Lillo, and Raymond. While walking by, someone would notice Curtis or Lillo strumming the instrument.

"Let me see that thing, boy! I haven't played a guitar in months."

"I didn't know you could play the guitar," Curtis would say.

"I sho' can. Gimme that thing and I'll show you."

A quick demonstration would prove that he, indeed, could play.

Our house on Mary Street was always full of singing. But the sound of guitars dominated. Daddy had a guitar and spent time strumming it and blowing on his harmonica. One year, he bought Lillo and Curtis acoustic guitars for Christmas. They played those guitars almost every day, especially Curtis. One day, Lamar Wells, the son of Miss Ella Lee, our next-door neighbor, came to visit his mother. After seeing Curtis and Lillo sitting on the porch playing their guitars, he came over.

"Y'all sound pretty good," he told them. "Y'all wanna play with my gospel group?"

The Northwest Gospel Singers was one of many gospel groups that performed at churches around the area. Recording stars like Sam Cooke and Lou Rawls were nurtured in groups like the Northwest Gospel Singers.

Curtis answered yes quickly and went to the group's practice. There were two electric guitars there, a lead and a bass. Robert Wyatt, the group's regular guitarist, could play both. But he preferred to play the bass and began teaching Curtis new chords on the lead guitar. A quick learner, Curtis joined the group that evening and was allowed to keep the electric guitar at home, where he practiced on it every day. He played not only for the Northwest Gospel Singers but also for other gospel groups that sought his musical talent. Influenced by the music they heard around them and on radio and television, Curtis and Lillo joined an R & B band when they were young teenagers. The group played venues around northern Louisiana. Raymond, a few years younger than Curtis and Lillo, learned to play bass guitar, too, and Lauriece and Elizabeth Ann sang with them.

Curtis, Lillo, Lauriece, and Raymond became professional singers, musicians, songwriters, and producers. They were part of the music-nurturing environment in Mansfield.

One day, I caught the musical spirit of the fifties. I saw an ad in a magazine that leaped out at me.

GET YOUR SONG RECORDED! JUST $15, it said.

I went to work writing a song that would one day be recorded by Little Richard or Fats Domino or Chuck Berry, I just knew it would!

> *I got a gal*
> *She's so fine.*
> *One thing about her—*
> *She's not mine.*
>
> *She's another man's baby.*
> *She's another man's baby.*
> *She's another man's baby because she's not mine.*

When I finished it, I knew my song was a hit. After writing the lyrics on lineless paper with a ballpoint pen, I placed it in an envelope along with a money order for fifteen dollars. I rushed to put the envelope in the mailbox before the mailman got there.

We lived just outside the city borders, so the mailman didn't deliver mail to our house. Daddy bought a small metal mailbox and perched it atop a thick pole he placed firmly in the ground at the end of the mailman's route on our street.

That's where we picked up our mail or placed letters we wanted to send out.

I watched the mailman pull my letter from the box and place it into his bag. Then, I waited. A week passed. Several weeks. A month. After several months, I gave up. *A hard lesson has been learned,* I thought. The fifteen dollars I had worked hard to earn had been lost. One day, however, I heard Madear say, "Brother, come here. A package came for you. I don't know what it is."

I opened it. There, in a manila envelope, wrapped loosely in thin paper, was a 45-rpm vinyl record. I pulled it from the small box slowly and looked at it carefully.

Emblazoned on the disc were the words "Another Man's Baby," the title of my song. "By Wade Hudson" was printed underneath it. As I stared at my name, I started thinking about what I was going to buy with the money I would earn when I sent my hit song to a record company to be recorded by a star. I'd buy a new house, a new car, a new television. I was going to buy Madear new clothes and get Christmas toys for all my brothers and sisters. I had it all planned.

Excitedly, I ran to the small record player Jurdine had just bought and nervously put the disc in place. I braced myself as the needle engaged the vinyl. As the record began to play, my heart sank.

It wasn't the song I had had in mind when I wrote the lyrics.

I wanted to stop the record from playing before anyone else could hear it. Instead of sounding like a song Little

Richard or Chuck Berry would record, it had Lawrence Welk big-band polka and waltz music written all over it, except with just a piano and a vocalist who had a country twang.

What was this? This wasn't the song I had written!

I wanted to take the disc and throw it as far as I could. I didn't want anybody to hear it. So, I placed it underneath the mattress in my bedroom. No one would find it there, I thought.

Radio disc jockeys often ran contests for listeners to help promote their programs. Questions would be asked about a current event, and the first person to call in with the correct answer received a gift.

One day, I knew the answer. We didn't have a telephone, so I ran across the street. Miss Teencha, Ray Bogan's grandmother, gave me permission to use her phone.

"Do you have the answer?" the DJ asked.

"Nineteen forty-five!" I shouted out.

"We have a winner! We have a winner! The United Nations was established in 1945. This smart young man knew the correct answer. Are you good in school, young man?"

"Yes, sir," I replied.

"Well, you stay on the line so we can tell you how to pick up your prize."

I waited for almost five minutes before a secretary came on the line to tell me I had won a portable radio that I had to pick up at the station. But Daddy wouldn't drive all the way to Shreveport for it. I had won, but I wouldn't get the prize.

Several weeks later, Miss Teencha came over to talk to my mother.

"Lurline," she said, holding a telephone bill in her hand, "I got this long-distance call to Shreveport on my bill. I think Brother made it when he asked to use the phone a few weeks ago."

"Lord have mercy. Miss Teencha, I'm so sorry," Madear apologized. "That boy know better than that. Brother, come here."

"Yes, Madear?"

"Did you make a call to Shreveport on Miss Teencha's phone?"

"I used the phone, but I didn't know it was long distance."

"Well, it is."

"That's all right, Lurline. He didn't know."

"But he should of asked me before runnin' over to your house to use the phone. Let me pay you for it."

Madear paid Miss Teencha for the phone call with money she needed for the family.

Another lesson was learned.

CHAPTER 11

Family Crisis

One late afternoon, Madear came running down the steps and into the yard where PG and I were playing. She had just received a call from someone at Daddy's job.

"It's always something!" she cried as she ran down the street. Jurdine ran out of the house, too.

"Daddy got hurt at the job," Jurdine told us. "He fell off a stack of logs. They say it's bad. Madear gone to get somebody to drive her to the hospital."

We didn't know whether our father was dead or alive. We all gathered in the living room—Jurdine; PG; Lillo; Curtis; Lauriece; Major, who was the baby; and I—and waited anxiously to hear some word.

I prayed a silent prayer, remembering the gospel song that had been playing when we first heard the news: "Did You Stop to Pray This Morning?"

The song by the Pilgrim Travelers blared loudly from the radio in our living room and served as a soundtrack all afternoon because the DJ played it over and over. I remember thinking, *Did Daddy's accident happen because I didn't stop to pray this morning?*

What if Daddy is dead?

What would we do without him?

Who would show me and PG baseball tips?

My mind raced ahead, full of so many questions.

When Madear came home hours later, she said Daddy had a badly broken leg, but that he would be okay.

"They gonna keep him for a few days so they can make sure the bones are set right. They said it was a bad break. Lord, if it ain't one thing, it's another."

Daddy came home several days later with a cast on his left leg that ran from his upper thigh to his ankle. It would take months for his leg to heal.

If you don't work, you don't get paid.

Black folks in Mansfield knew what that meant. And we would find out how it would devastate our family. Daddy couldn't work. Madear couldn't either, because having so many children had taken a toll on her physically.

Like most Black people in Mansfield, we had had tough times before, but we'd been able to "keep moving," as folks described surviving. We were able to hang in there until things got better. But this period of trouble tested us beyond our ability to even understand it.

Ma'am Ma helped as best she could. Occasionally, Uncle

Buddy sent money to help. There were times when the electricity and gas service were terminated. Somehow, though, Madear almost always found a way to get the service turned on again. She would go to the utility company's office and plead her case. Sometimes she convinced them to accept partial payment from money she had borrowed. Other times she just made a case for mercy and the service was restored.

There were times when there was no food. Sometimes, Madear would write a note for PG and me to take to the local grocery store where she shopped. She was always able to touch others' hearts with her words. I am sure in the note she requested an extension to her bill and listed food items she needed. The White owner would read the note, then ask us to wait. PG and I looked at the shelves full of pastries, cakes, cookies, and other foods as the grocer filled several large bags with food and gave them to us. PG and I struggled with them as we walked home.

Often, our first meal was lunch at school. If we didn't have the five cents to pay for it, we got it from Ma'am Ma.

One morning, a station wagon pulled into the driveway. Bob Johnson, a short man with a thick mustache, slid out and held the car door open.

"You boys come here and take this food into the house," he directed us.

By then, Madear had come to the front door.

"What's this, Bob?" she asked, a quizzical look on her face.

"What does it look like, Lurline?" Mr. Johnson answered pointedly. "I'm bringing y'all some food. Y'all should have let somebody know how y'all struggling. We here to help each other. That's what we do."

He continued to direct us just as he did those who worked at the funeral home he managed.

"Don't drop that bag. It's got eggs in it. Where's Wade?" he asked Madear.

"He hobbled over to see his mother. You didn't buy all this yourself, did you, Bob?" Madear asked, seeing bag after bag of food being taken into the house.

"Some of it. The Masonic boys chipped in. We wouldn't have known y'all were going hungry if June Henderson hadn't told us. He's a Mason, too, you know."

Mr. Johnson wasn't a native of Mansfield. He had moved to town to help manage the local branch of his brother Ben's chain of funeral homes. Ben Johnson established his first funeral home in 1932, and by the 1950s, he had them in other towns and cities in Louisiana, as well as an insurance company. His business acumen enabled him to become one of the richest Black persons in the state.

"Wade Jr.," Mr. Johnson called to me.

"Yes, sir, Mr. Bob," I answered, picking up the last bag of food.

"I hear how smart you are in school. We're going to start a Knights of Pythagoras chapter soon and I want you to be one of the first to join."

"What's the Knights of Pythagoras?" I asked.

"It's a junior chapter of the Masons. I'll tell you more about it later."

"Yes, sir. I'm interested."

Bob got back into his station wagon, closed the door, then leaned his head out the window.

"Lurline," he called to Madear, who was still standing in the doorway.

"Y'all take care of yourselves, you hear. And tell Wade I wanna talk to him."

"I will, Bob. Thank you again!" Madear had tears in her eyes.

Later that day, June Henderson, Cleonis's father, came to the house. Daddy had returned from visiting Ma'am Ma. As soon as he entered the house, Mr. June walked right up to my father.

"Wade, don't you ever let your family go hungry, you hear me! We're here to help each other. Y'all done helped others. Why can't you let us help you?"

"June, we didn't wanna be no trouble to anybody. Everybody got problems."

After his answer my father looked away, as if he wanted to disappear.

"That's bullshit, Wade! None of us should be too proud to ask for help. You got growing children here, a house full of 'em. Them children shouldn't go hungry."

"Yeah, you right, June. You right." Daddy tried to force a smile. "You won't git no more argument from me."

Mr. June placed a comforting hand on my father's shoulder. A hefty man with a bulging belly, Mr. June, like Bob

Johnson, was one of the men in the community that we looked up to, that we respected, and to whom we listened when they spoke. It was these men's obligation to safeguard the community as best they could and to protect the children.

"If there is anything we can do, you let us know," he told Daddy. "We can't help you if we don't know."

"Thank you, June. We sho' appreciate it." Daddy accepted his handshake and escorted Mr. June to the door.

"God bless you, June!" my mother shouted to him as he walked down the steps. "God bless you."

Madear was a fighter, continuously pushing to find answers to problems. She never gave up, was never willing to accept defeat. She always searched for a way out. Her unyielding spirit was always front and center.

Daddy was different. He cared, too. I knew that. But something seemed to be missing. A hard worker, he faithfully assumed his responsibilities as the primary breadwinner. But when situations got difficult, he withdrew. Madear was the one who plunged in for the rescue.

I don't think my father was always laid back like that. There had to have been a time when he, too, had that tenacious spirit, that never-give-up willpower. He, too, at one point, must have believed that the struggle, the striving, was worth it and that there was no other alternative. The faith of our ancestors was a part of him, too. They believed "The Lord Will Make a Way Somehow," no matter how difficult the challenge.

Did Daddy lose that fire, that drive, that never-give-up spirit when he was a young boy growing up in a White-dominated society determined to keep him from becoming a man? Maybe he held on for a while but lost it when he went into the army and his expectations were smashed and he was forced to realize that "Mansfield" was everywhere. Maybe he lost it when he returned home to the same racist system he had left. Maybe after going to mechanics' school on the GI Bill, starting a small mechanics' shop from scratch with a partner and seeing it burn down in a suspicious fire was just too much to endure. Maybe he just settled into acceptance, with his aspirations squashed. Or maybe, maybe it was just the way he was wired, the way he was. Whatever the reason, he didn't have the fight, the tenacity that Madear had.

After Daddy recovered from his broken leg, he found a job again as a common laborer, the only work available to him. He settled into his early-morning and late-evening work regimen again.

Then, another crisis hit the family! The mounting responsibilities added up and Madear succumbed to them. She began to feel weak and dizzy. The doctor said she had low blood pressure. That slowed her down. Always talkative and lively, she became withdrawn and wanted to be left alone. She remained in her room often, sometimes with the covers pulled over her head. She didn't cook very much then. Jurdine did that, and sometimes Daddy cooked when he came home from work.

That wasn't the Madear I knew.

"Y'all keep quiet around her," Aunt Essie told us. "Don't disturb your mother. She isn't well."

"What's wrong, Aunt Essie?" I inquired, extremely concerned.

"Lurline just isn't well, that's all. She'll be all right in a little while," my aunt replied.

We listened and did our best so that our mother could get well.

Sometimes, I went into her room and just stared at her while she slept.

We wanted our old Madear back and did everything we could to make that possible. One day I even yelled at Aunt Margaret when she sought to disturb Madear.

"Leave her alone!" I insisted. "She resting!"

"You too mannish, Brother. I just wanna ask Lurline something."

Aunt Margaret always played the youngest-child-in-the-family role to the fullest. And Madear let her have her way. She had been just a baby when Grandma Shug died, so Madear always felt sorry for her. She used to say, "I'm the only mother Margaret ever knew. She never knew her own mother like the rest of us did."

But I had to protect my own mother.

"Y'all too forward," Margaret complained, giving up. "Brother, you just as mannish as you wanna be. Lurline and Wade got y'all spoiled rotten. I'm leaving anyway."

No one ever said the name of Madear's illness. They just

said she wasn't well or didn't feel good. After several months, she bounced back and was her old self again. Then, her "not well" period would return. This on-and-off health struggle continued for several years.

During this time, I started writing poems and short stories. I don't remember why I started writing. I didn't see writers around me. Writing became like breathing for me. It was something I *had* to do. I wrote poems about nature, the weather, people I saw, school. I wrote stories about finding money and using my good fortune to help my family. I wrote down the ghost stories my mother told us.

At first, I wrote on single sheets of paper that Madear kept for writing letters to Uncle Buddy in Houston. But I would lose what I had written. So, I bought a pad of paper from Mr. James Root's corner store. It became my poetry book. When I wasn't playing sports with my friends, I could usually be found sitting on the steps of our front porch, writing something.

"What ya doing, Brother, sitting there all by yourself?" someone would ask.

"Writing," I would answer.

"Ya mean a letter?"

"No, a poem," I'd say.

"A poem?"

"Yes, ma'am."

"What you gonna do with a poem?" she asked.

"I don't know. I just feel like writing it, that's all," I replied.

"Lord have mercy! A poem."

Sometimes, someone such as Mrs. Ella Henderson, Cleonis's mother, stopped and asked me to let her read what I had written.

"You wrote this?" she asked after reading one of my poems.

"Yes, ma'am, I wrote it. I just wrote it."

"You sho' you didn't copy it from a book?" Mrs. Henderson asked.

"No, ma'am! No, ma'am! I wrote it myself."

Mrs. Ella just looked at me.

"I don't think Lurline and Wade know what a smart boy they got. This is a good poem."

During one of his sermons, Reverend M. B. Collins, the pastor of our church, said that we all had gifts that God gave out generously to everyone. I thought God's gifts had given me the ability to write down what I was thinking. Ma'am Ma thought so, too. Whenever I gave her one of my poems to read, she made a big deal out of it.

"Look at this! Just look at this!" Ma'am Ma would exclaim.

If someone was nearby, she would show it to him or her.

"Look at what my grandson wrote. Ain't that something?"

Rarely did I show my writing to my parents. Perhaps I thought they were too busy to pay attention to it. They always had so much to do to provide for us. Nor did I offer teachers at school opportunities to read my written work. I read them to my siblings, but thought they were too young to appreciate them. I just continued to write, not knowing what would happen to what I had written. Words and ideas would come to me and I would write them down. Sometimes they didn't make much sense. Often the grammar needed work. Every once in a while, though, a poem leaped off the page and I felt good about it.

As I progressed through each grade in elementary school, I paid close attention to the poets in our English textbooks—Robert Frost, Carl Sandburg, and Emily Dickinson. Novels, too, usually excerpted, by Mark Twain, Herman Melville, Nathaniel Hawthorne, and Robert Louis Stevenson. But there were no Black writers in those English textbooks. No Langston Hughes, Zora Neale Hurston, Richard Wright, or Gwendolyn Brooks. Every new school year I searched the English textbooks, hoping to find something written by a Black writer. Or even a story or poem about Black people. But my search was always futile. After finally giving up, I was determined that one day, *I* would be included in one of those textbooks.

Throughout high school, I continued to write. I never considered becoming a professional writer. That was a profession I saw only White people pursuing. My parents and some of my teachers encouraged me to become a teacher, a safe career for Black people who had the fortunate opportunity to attend college.

CHAPTER 12

A Team of Our Own

I read the sports pages of the daily newspaper as often as I could. I wanted to know who had won the games the day before and how my favorite players had performed. In those newspapers, I saw coverage of sports played by White kids my age. There were basketball leagues and Little League baseball teams. Pictures of these boys clad in their uniforms were right there among the photos of professional teams. *Why don't we have organized sports like them?* I wondered. Where were our sports leagues and teams?

We had only the plot of land next to Mr. and Mrs. Lee's house where we could play baseball. Mr. and Mrs. Blow's lawn served us well, but it wasn't a real football field like the one the White kids had.

One day in early June of 1958, I declared that we were going to start our own summer baseball program and we were going to play on the field at DeSoto Parish Training School.

I organized a few of the neighborhood boys and we went knocking on doors.

"Hi, Miss Ella. We trying to raise money to buy equipment so we can start our own baseball team. Can you give us a donation?" we asked.

"You boys something else. You gonna start your own team, you say?"

"Yes, ma'am. The White boys got their teams. Why shouldn't we have our own, too?" we said.

"Yes, y'all something, all right. Let me see if I got some change." Miss Ella reached into her apron pocket and pulled out a dollar.

"Here, take this. And don't waste it, now," she told us.

"We won't. Thank you very much."

We received similar responses wherever we went.

"What you gonna buy with the money?"

"Some balls and bats and other baseball stuff," we said.

"Well, I rather see y'all doing something good instead of gittin' in trouble. Here's seventy-five cents. This should help a little. Wish I had more, but you just caught me at the wrong time."

"This is great! This will help a lot!"

After a while, we had enough money to purchase bats, baseballs, a catcher's mitt, and a catcher's breast protector.

Late one afternoon, when it was not too hot, we made our way to the DeSoto Parish Training School and staked out our baseball field. It was just us, the boys from the east side, mostly from Mary Street. I was eleven years old and had taken one of my first steps of leadership. This was our team:

First base: Cleonis Henderson

Second base: Li'l Ray Woodley

Shortstop: me

Third base: James Ray Bogan

Left field: Elijah "Crow" Williams

Center field: Butch Brantley

Right field: Willie James Haley

Catcher: PG

Pitcher: Vida Blue

Vida was younger than most of us. He lived down the street, next door to Cleonis, his first cousin. Vida held his own against the older boys. He was like a brother to us Hudson boys, often dropping by our house to hang out and enjoy the tea cakes Madear baked.

Every late afternoon around four o'clock we played baseball together, teaching ourselves the fundamentals of the game. We practiced making double plays, learning how to bunt, and making up signs just like they did in the major league. Sometimes Daddy dropped by after work to give us tips. Other men, like Mr. "Fats" Brown, who had played semi-professionally, came to offer advice. Mostly, however, it was just us, learning and playing the game we loved and the game that we, one day, would play in the major league just like Jackie Robinson, Hank Aaron, Willie Mays, and Ernie Banks had done.

We didn't have permission to use the field at the school. We were afraid that once we were seen by school administrators we would be told to leave. So, whenever we saw someone coming from the school building toward us, we became anxious. But no one ever stopped us. We played all summer.

Toward the end of the following year a large metal screen was assembled right behind the catcher's area, where PG was always positioned. We didn't know what to make of it.

Unbeknownst to us, the school administration had decided to support our summer baseball program and had assigned W. F. Jones, a former football star at DeSoto, to oversee it. That first day, he brought a large bag filled with baseballs, bats, bases, and catcher's equipment. We were in baseball heaven.

A Wednesday evening softball program was organized for adults, too. The games were played under lights that had been erected because of the success of the high school championship football team. That team won state titles in 1956, 1957, and 1958. Some of us wondered if our taking the initiative to start our own baseball program had inspired the Wednesday evening adult program, too.

That summer, we began competing against a team from another part of Black Mansfield called the Kansas City Sub-Division. The name was derived from the Kansas City Southern train line that ran near the area. Several times a week, our teams played each other. Sometimes we played against a team from South Mansfield.

Vida was our primary pitcher. Jesse Hudson was the main pitcher for KCS. Both were outstanding even at their young ages. Sometimes our games ended scoreless because no one could hit off of either one of them. If our team won, it was usually because the other team had made errors. If they won, we had made errors. Vida and Jesse had blazing fastballs that few players could swing fast enough at to hit. We were happy when Jesse didn't pitch, and they were elated when Vida didn't.

In high school football, Vida and Jesse teamed up to be just as unbeatable. Vida was the star quarterback, throwing thirty-five touchdown passes in one season. Jesse caught seventeen of those passes. It was baseball, however, that provided both the opportunity to leave Mansfield and our summer league competition that helped to prepare them.

Around four o'clock every summer afternoon, if you looked down Mary Street, you would see the Mary Street Boys, Vida and Cleonis walking, carrying their baseball gloves. Ray Bogan would meet them. PG and I usually stood on the porch waiting for them. Together we made the two-mile walk to the baseball field to gather with the guys from our side of town to participate in our favorite sport.

DeSoto had not had a high school baseball team since the early 1950s. It was the players from our summer baseball program that brought the game back and established it as a major sport at DeSoto High School.

CHAPTER 13

Churchgoing Time

In July, my baseball season was rudely interrupted. It was time for me to join church and accept Jesus Christ as my Savior. I would turn twelve in October, the age of responsibility, church folks said, when an adolescent should know the difference between right and wrong and could make a personal decision to accept Christ. There was no debating it. By twelve years of age, a youngster had to go to revival and sit on the mourner's bench.

Revival at Elizabeth Baptist Church Number Three, our family church, began on a Monday. I was devastated because I wouldn't be able to play in any baseball games while the revival was being held.

Who would take my position at shortstop? Who would keep the statistics? Who would teach the guys the rules of the game? Because I read every baseball book I could get my hands on, I knew a lot about the game. Who would replace me? More important, I just wanted to be able to play the game I dreamed about almost every night during the summer.

That Monday, I stood in the doorway and watched my teammates start their daily trip to the baseball field. I didn't say a word as PG joined them. In fact, my brother hadn't said a word to me all day about baseball or hardly anything else. Sitting on the mourner's bench during revival required commitment, focus, and opening oneself to receive the Holy Spirit.

"Don't play with God!" the old folks said. "If you want to let Jesus Christ in to be your Lord and Savior, you gotta move everything else out of the way. You gotta let him have his way."

That meant no television, no books, no playing games, no baseball, and no breathing, if it got in the way.

At around 5:30, my great-uncle Jamie, Papa's baby brother, came to get me in his old pickup truck. The cab was already filled with his family, so I sat in the back with three or four others.

"You ready?" Uncle Jamie asked before pulling off.

"Yes, sir," I answered.

"I'm glad you on the mourner's bench. We need more young people in the church."

"Yes, sir."

As the wind blew on my face during the five-mile drive, I wondered what it would be like to sit on the mourner's bench. And why did they call it a mourner's bench? *Maybe because until you are saved, you are in mourning,* I thought. That answer was as good as any.

When the truck pulled up in the gravel driveway in front of the old, wood-framed building, I got nervous. My hands trembled so much, I almost lost my balance when I leaped from the back of the truck.

As I approached the steps of the church, I noticed that the aging front door had been replaced. Like so many Black churches in the area, Elizabeth Number Three had been built mostly by extended family members and friends. These dedicated members also did the work to maintain it.

We were early. Uncle Jamie opened the door and escorted me to the front pew on the left side of the church, the one designated as the mourner's bench. He raised all the windows and picked up any paper on the floor that the sexton had overlooked.

"It's hot now, but it's gonna get hotter when more people git in here," Uncle Jamie said to no one in particular as he continued looking for trash to remove. "Some folks are still gettin' off work."

Before long, around thirty people had gathered and the revival began. One of the deacons kneeled in front of his pew and prayed. Then, a single female voice burst into song. There were no instruments, but that didn't matter. The voice filled the church as the others listened intently.

I heard the voice of Jesus say, come unto me and rest.

When she finished the first line of the old hymn, the congregation joined her, repeating what she had just sung. Each person embraced the words in their own way, stretching them to emote their own feeling and meaning. It all blended, though, into one big choir sound that made me tremble and brought tears to my eyes. Tears rolled down the faces of others, too.

Lay down, thou weary one, lay down thy head upon my breast.

The leader's voice rose again. Having been led properly, the congregation followed as it had done with the first line. The Holy Spirit had now taken over.

When the congregational singing ended, Reverend M. B. Collins, a portly man with several gold front teeth, a friendly, engaging smile, and processed hair, walked slowly to the pulpit. He announced the subject of his sermon, and for the remainder of the evening, he preached to the five of us seated on the mourner's bench. After delivering a stirring sermon, he was drenched in perspiration. But none of us accepted his invitation to join church.

By the end of the evening, I realized that accepting Jesus Christ and joining church was serious business. The hymns and sermon had touched me and captured my attention. I forgot about baseball, and that night, before going to bed, I prayed that Jesus would save my soul.

The members of the church who had been "walking with the Lord for a long time" said that when you're really saved, God always sends a sign. Some shared their conversion experience, comparing it to the apostle Paul's vision on the road to Damascus, when he was struck blind when God "called" him.

All that first week, I prayed and waited for the sign. I prayed in the morning. Sometimes while I was in the yard alone, I prayed. I prayed before I went to sleep. But I didn't see or feel a sign like the old people talked about.

"Don't bother Brother. Leave him alone. He's trying to get his soul saved," Madear told my brothers and sisters. And no one did. I almost felt abandoned.

The second week came. Still no sign.

One night while it was raining, I went into the backyard and looked up. A bolt of lightning flashed across the sky and thunder soon followed. It was obvious that it would rain for a while, perhaps all night, according to the weather forecast.

"God," I called out, "if my soul is saved, show me a sign! Let it stop raining. Let it stop lightning and thundering."

I waited for the rain to stop. I continued to wait as it drenched me, the water running down my face and soaking my clothes. The lightning continued to streak across the sky and thunder continued to roar. No sign!

On a clear night with no hint of rain, when the stars sparkled and the moon shone brightly, I again looked up into the sky, where I assumed God was, and said, "God, if you have saved my soul, let me know by sending the rain, a bolt of lightning, and thunder!"

Still, nothing happened.

Was I going to get my sign like Paul got his?

By Wednesday, people started whispering.

"It won't be this year. He's gonna have to come back next year."

"Reverend Collins really preaching, though. Them others joined. Ain't too much more Reverend Collins can do. Wade and Lurline's boy is hard to reach."

"He'll move when the Spirit say 'move,'" Reverend Collins said, chastising the gossipers.

On Friday, the last night of the revival, I sat on the mourner's bench alone. Seated in his chair near the pulpit, Reverend Collins looked tired. It had been a long two weeks. Church members called it a successful revival. Four people had become Christians and increased the church membership. But I could see Reverend Collins wasn't satisfied. There was still one who was not in the fold. He looked straight at me. A caring expression on his face helped me relax.

"Lord, where is the sign?" I whispered. "Where is the sign?"

The last night of church revivals usually drew the most people. Some came to see how it would end. Others came to see who had joined church. Ma'am Ma was there. So were other assorted relatives.

The service began, a deacon prayed, the congregation sang, and Reverend Collins preached. After finishing, he offered his hand to me. He had done that every night. But every night I had sat staring at the floor, avoiding his probing eyes. I sat there as my fellow mourners rose and accepted his invitation. I sat there as he stood in front of me, waiting for me, too, to give him my hand. But I never did. Nine nights had passed and there I was, sitting alone on the mourner's bench!

But something happened that last night. As the congregation sang its final hymn, Reverend Collins stood before me holding out his hand, and something happened. My body began to tremble and perspiration ran down my face like small beads of rain. Suddenly, I leaped from that mourner's bench! It was as if something had yanked me and pulled me forward. Without realizing it, I had given my hand to Reverend Collins, who now wore a broad smile.

"Praise the Lord!" I heard someone shout. "Praise him!"

Quickly, others joined in the celebration. Madear had been seated behind me almost every night of the revival. I heard her voice over everyone else's.

"Thank you, Lord! Thank you, Lord! Thank you, Lord!"

And the thank-you-Lords just kept on coming.

Out of the corner of my eye, I saw Ma'am Ma leap up from her seat and rush toward me. Overcome with joy, she jumped up and down as if she was riding a pogo stick. When she reached me, she began pounding me with her closed hands.

"Somebody git her!" Deacon Walter Taylor directed one of the ushers. "She's got the Holy Ghost. She don't know what she's doing. She gonna hurt that boy."

Reverend Collins tried to protect me as best he could. Two ushers came over and led my grandmother back to her seat.

I had done it! I had accepted Jesus Christ! I had become a Christian!

Everyone in the church was happy that my soul would be saved from eternal damnation in hell. I was happy, too—glad that God had shown me the sign at last by using the Holy Spirit to push me up from that mourner's bench.

That Sunday, I awoke early. I was going to be baptized and

would be welcomed into the church officially. Madear had already prepared breakfast, but I didn't feel hungry. I was nervous, anticipating what was going to happen within a few hours. What would it be like to be baptized, to be dipped in the water, head and all? Suppose something happened? Suppose Reverend Collins and Deacon Taylor slipped, or lost their balance? What would I do? I didn't know how to swim.

"Brother, you ready?" yelled Madear from the kitchen.

"Yes, I'm ready. I'm puttin' on my clothes now," I answered from my bedroom.

"You better eat something."

"I ain't hungry."

"It's gonna be a long day. They'll have food there, but you won't be able to eat until late in the day."

"I'm just not hungry now."

I finished dressing and walked to the front porch, where I stood watching the sun beginning to make its impact on the day. Soon, we headed to church.

Baptisms always took place before the service began. I went into the church, found a secluded space, and changed from my black suit into blue jeans and a T-shirt. A deacon gave me a white robe that I put on over the jeans and T-shirt. The other candidates for baptism and I were escorted to a pond about a half mile from the church. When we arrived, people were already there, surrounding the small body of water, waiting for the baptism to start.

Reverend Collins, Deacon Taylor, and another deacon waded into the pond until they reached the center, where the water came up to their knees. Deacon Taylor offered one of the emotional prayers for which he was known and one by one, the candidates for baptism were brought to the pastor to be submerged in the murky water. When my turn came, two deacons led me to the center of the pond.

"Relax and hold your breath," Reverend Collins told me. He knew I was anxious. "It'll be all right," he added, trying to reassure me.

He placed his large left hand behind my head, each deacon grabbed one of my shoulders, and they took control of my entire body. I could hear the people who had come to witness one of the most important ordinances in the Baptist church, singing "Take Me to the Water."

> *Take me to the water*
> *Take me to the water*
> *Take me to the water*
> *To be baptized.*

"Do you accept Jesus Christ as your Lord and Savior?" Reverend Collins asked me in a loud voice so others could hear. I looked down at the cold water, wondering what it was going to feel like to have my clothes and my body drenched in it.

"I do," I answered.

With his left hand still cradling the back of my head, he raised his right hand toward the sky.

"I baptize you in the name of the Father, the Son, and the Holy Ghost!"

In one quick, concerted movement the three church leaders plunged me into the water and brought me up again. I had been baptized! I shook my head to get rid of some of the water. The worshippers, now caught up in the excitement, moved on to the next line of the song, singing it with even more enthusiasm and sprinkling in applause, hallelujahs, and amens. Deacon Taylor gave me a towel to wipe the water from my face.

> *I love Jesus.*
> *I love Jesus.*
> *I love Jesus.*
> *Yes, I do!*

After arriving at the church again, I pulled off the wet clothes and exchanged them for my black suit. During the service that followed, Reverend Collins delivered another moving sermon. After he finished, the new members, including me, stood in the front of the church. People came up to shake our hands. It was our official welcome as members of Elizabeth Baptist Church Number Three. The day continued with an abundance of food and fellowship. It didn't end until nearly five o'clock. But it was a typical day of baptism, one that our church observed just like all the other Black churches in Mansfield.

On Monday, I was happy to rejoin my baseball teammates. They were happy to see me, too. Two weeks is a long time in baseball.

But I was also happy that I had given my life to Jesus Christ. I took it seriously, too. I began to read the Bible regularly, prayed often, and became involved in the life of the church.

The members of Elizabeth Number Three embraced me. Reverend Collins, the deacons, and church leaders took me under their wings. With fewer than one hundred members, Elizabeth's congregation was mostly older members who had struggled all their lives as sharecroppers and laborers. Some couldn't read or write. Although I was barely in my teens, they included me in their important meetings and sought my advice. I learned to pray before the congregation. My first speaking opportunities were at Elizabeth. If there was jealousy over my youth, I never saw it. Those church people helped me mature in so many ways—Reverend M. B. Collins, Deacon Taylor, Brother Eddie Jones, and so many others. I remember them all.

CHAPTER 14

A New School

I couldn't wait to start the seventh grade. Mr. Blow, our neighbor across the street, the one with the big lawn for playing football on, was going to be my teacher. I knew I was going to be special in his class. He was my friend. Sometimes, he paid PG and me to cut his lawn. We did other errands for him, too.

Then I found out that I wouldn't be attending DeSoto. Instead, I would be attending Johnson Elementary School in South Mansfield for my seventh-grade school year. And the students that had been transferred would have to ride a bus to get there.

Why me? I wondered. Why did my seventh-grade class have to change schools? Why did I have to go all the way to South Mansfield? I didn't even know where that was. PG didn't have to go. Why me?

Going to school at Johnson Elementary meant I had to

get up early in the morning, walk for fifteen minutes to the DeSoto Parish Training School campus, and then catch a bus for the ride to South Mansfield.

Mr. Blow probably won't be my teacher, I thought. *I'll get a teacher from Johnson Elementary that I don't even know.*

When I walked to DeSoto that first morning to catch the bus, I didn't know what to expect. Since the first grade I had been classmates with Wanda Faye Hudson, David Jones, my cousin Lois Woodley, Earnie Marie Washington, Frank Pea, Tom Reed, Joe Curtis Pugh, and Willie Louis Davis. Some of them were on the school bus, too. But would they be my classmates?

Johnson Elementary was a newly built brick building unlike DeSoto Parish Training School's old painted wooden structures. At Johnson Elementary, the big windows could be pushed outward for fresh air. Heat came from vents. The floors were tiled. And students didn't have to go outside to use the toilets. Restrooms were inside the building. Johnson Elementary looked more like a school for White students than the more cheaply constructed buildings to which most Black people were accustomed.

I was relieved that I had the same classmates as before, including Wanda Faye. Mr. Blow was our teacher, too.

At first, I missed old DeSoto. I missed the sound of the large bell that rang in the morning to start classes and in the afternoon to signal the end of the school day. I even missed the old green building. But after a while, I was a Johnsonite.

I had assumed that because Mr. Blow was my neighbor and I did chores for him sometimes he would be easy on me in the classroom. I was wrong.

Mr. Blow knew I had been getting by on my reputation as a smart student, and that I hadn't really been motivated to achieve as I should. So, he pushed me. Because he lived across the street, he knew when I was playing instead of doing my homework. Sometimes when we played in his yard, he would tell us it was time to go home.

"Tomorrow is a school day," he would tell us.

He introduced classroom contests to spur all of us to compete with one another.

One day during math class, he called David Jones and me to the front of the classroom. David and I were both good math students. While Mr. Blow wrote two math problems on the blackboard, he had us look away. When he had finished, he told us to solve the problems. I knew the answer without using the blackboard to calculate it. While David was still working on his answer, I wrote mine on the blackboard in a matter of seconds. Mr. Blow leaped to his feet.

"That's amazing! That's amazing," he kept repeating. "How did you solve that problem so fast, neighbor?" He pulled a desk to the front of the room not far from his own desk and pointed at it.

"Sit there! You're king for a day! You see how fast he answered that, class?"

Mr. Blow gave one of the students a dollar and asked her to purchase a soda and pack of cookies. When she returned, he had her give the treats to me. I had never experienced anything like that kind of recognition in a classroom before. I was a superstar!

Throughout the school year, Mr. Blow challenged us and pushed us in all our classes. His animated teaching style engaged us and sometimes made us laugh. In class, he seldom referred to me as Wade.

"Neighbor, you know the answer?"

"You have your hand up. What do you say, neighbor?"

"That's the answer, neighbor. That's it!"

I really enjoyed my seventh-grade school year at Johnson Elementary. Because of Mr. Blow, I learned to appreciate friendly classroom academic competition.

CHAPTER 15

An Incident to Remember

After I finished seventh grade, PG and I got our first real jobs, thanks to Mr. Greenard, the agriculture teacher at the high school. He knew our family needed the extra money. So when summer jobs at the high school became available, he thought of us first.

"I'm glad," PG said, beaming. "We'll have full-time jobs this summer."

"Yeah. We can use the money. And we can still mow yards on Saturdays, too," I replied.

Our workday started at 8:30 a.m. and ended at 3:30 p.m., with a break for lunch. Our responsibilities included picking up trash on the campus, mowing the grass, and other assorted jobs Mr. Greenard assigned to us. The school campus was huge, so we stayed busy. We were excited when we received our first monthly paychecks—$62.00 minus Social Security and a few other deductions we didn't quite understand.

But this wasn't our first venture in earning money. We had

mowed lawns in the neighborhood, picked wild blackberries, raked leaves, and picked pecans for White families that Ma'am Ma worked for.

Once, PG and I were hired to help cultivate the lawn of a house in an all-White housing subdivision that had just been built. When we arrived, we were greeted by a mound of soil almost as tall as we were. We were to spread the soil evenly on the lawn so grass could be planted.

It must have been a hundred degrees on that hot summer day. We started in mid-morning, and as noon approached, the hot sun had nearly drained us. We were thirsty for water, our mouths nearly parched from lack of it, but there wasn't any.

Suddenly overcome by the heat, I dropped the shovel I was holding and hit the ground with a thud. Seconds later, PG did, too. We both lay on the ground for a while, passed out from dehydration. When we finally came to, we both wondered what had happened. When the man who hired us finally came back, he gave us water. But he was so disappointed because we had stopped working, he ushered us into his car and took us home.

"You boys ain't good for much," he complained. "I lost a whole day."

We didn't say anything. When we got out of the car, he sped off. He didn't even pay us for the work we had already done.

With the money PG and I earned doing our job at the school, we bought our own school clothes and helped buy them for our siblings, too. We bought food to help the family.

We kept some money for ourselves, too, to buy snacks, sports books, and magazines. *Playboy* magazine was the rage. Sometimes PG bought one. Sometimes I did. Finding a quiet place where no one could see us, we stared at the nude women who filled the pages of the publication that grown-ups called dirty and filthy. It wasn't dirty or filthy to us.

We didn't go downtown alone very often. When PG and I didn't go together, one of us was joined by other friends from the neighborhood. Numbers couldn't ensure our safety, but being alone meant even more danger lurked. One day, I did go alone to deposit my paycheck into my account at Mansfield Bank and Trust.

Usually when we walked downtown, we took the shortest route that passed our school. This time, I chose a different one. I walked up Mary Street and turned right onto Louise Street. After walking for about fifteen minutes, I prepared to turn left onto Polk Street, the main stretch that led to the downtown area. There, in the bend of the turn, sat a church that had an all-White congregation, of course. I had passed it often when riding the city bus or in my father's car. On a few Sundays, I had even seen its all-White members filing out and walking to their cars following the church service.

Like many of the White churches in Mansfield, this church was a well-built brick structure that stood out in the small town filled mostly with older wooden buildings. In our church, the God we knew was a God of all people. "Whosoever will, let him come" was a part of Scripture that was often lifted up.

But there were no White people in Elizabeth Number Three's congregation. We wouldn't have turned them away if they had come. On the other hand, a Black person could be arrested for trying to attend a service at a White church. So we viewed White Baptists from a distance, wondering if their God was the same as ours.

Just as I reached the church, three White boys rushed from the back of the church to the sidewalk.

"Do you know where Mango is?" shouted one of them.

Caught by surprise, nervously, I asked, *"Who?"*

"You heard me, n——? Do you know where Mango is?" The question was fired from his mouth like a bullet from a gun.

"I don't know him," I replied, hoping my answer would be enough and I could go on my way.

"You better know him, li'l n——! Or we'll beat your peanut head in!"

All three were built like linemen on the Mansfield High School football team, with muscular arms and broad shoulders. But the one with the big mouth was the biggest.

As I stood there, I thought about the stories I had heard of Black people being killed by White people for no reason at all. I thought about Emmett Till being lynched in Mississippi, allegedly for offending a White woman. I thought about the advice Madear gave so often. "Trouble easy to get into. Be careful. Stay in your place."

I rarely saw White people because all my young life I had lived on the east side, the Black section of town. The mailman was White. The bus driver was White. Sometimes White people came to Ma'am Ma's house to drop off work for her to do. But that was it.

I could count on one hand the number of White kids my age that I had seen. A few times White teenagers had sped past in their cars, yelling "n——" at us and calling us other foul names while giving us the finger. But they had never stopped to confront me.

Now I was about to have my first direct encounter with racism, and I was frightened. *Maybe I should run,* I thought. But how far could I get? This church was in the White section of town but not far from streets where Black people lived. If I was seen running, some White person might think I had done something bad and call the police. That could be worse.

The boys stood there glaring at me, waiting for me to give them an answer. They seemed ready to pound me into the ground, at the least, if I didn't give them one.

But I couldn't give them one! I didn't know the person they were asking about. I wouldn't have told them even if I did know where he was.

"We waiting, n——!" the big one said, walking closer toward me.

I didn't know what to do. I was a tall, skinny boy not yet in my teens. They were more like men.

Suddenly, I saw them step back and then move quickly toward the church. The smallest one quickened his pace and then began to run.

I looked around, wondering what was happening. Up the

sidewalk, about twenty yards away, I saw several Black teen-agers approaching. The White boys had spotted them. When I turned to see where they were, they had disappeared behind the church.

I was never so happy to see Black people in my life. I breathed a sigh of relief as they approached.

"Everything okay?" one of them asked.

"Yes, everything cool," I answered.

I didn't tell them what had happened. I don't know why. I just didn't. Maybe I was afraid I would get them in trouble if they confronted the young Ku Klux Klan. But it was obvi-ous to me that the White boys were cowards. They needed a larger number of them to work up the courage to attack more than one Black kid.

But that incident shook me. What would those White boys have done if those Black teenagers had not come along?

The confrontation made me angry, but I never told my family about it. I thought about it less as the activities of sum-mer filled up the days and weeks. It was baseball season and we had games to win.

CHAPTER 16

The Wedding of the Year

In late 1958, Jurdine and her boyfriend, John Adkins, announced they were getting married in March of the next year. Mr. and Mrs. Blow insisted that the wedding be held at their house.

Jurdine and John had been dating for more than a year. John lived on a small farm with his family in the rural area of the parish, but he had a car. While still going to high school, he worked at night at a lumber company in Mansfield. So most of his weekdays were full. On weekends, however, he came to court my sister. Sometimes, he and Jurdine would sit in the living room watching TV for hours. Like most parents during that time, Madear and Daddy were strict, especially Madear. They would not allow Jurdine and John to go anywhere alone. When they went to the store or downtown to buy something, either PG or I, and often both of us, went with them against my sister's protests.

"Madear, John's going to take me to the store to pick up a few things."

"Where's Brother? Tell Brother to get in here." I was summoned.

"We just going to the store, Madear. We'll be right back," my sister said.

"The devil is busy, child. Brother's going with y'all. He ain't gonna git in the way."

"Madear, you don't trust me and John," Jurdine complained.

"I don't trust the devil! Brother, go with 'em." Madear's word was final.

PG and I loved it. We had chances to go to places we would not have visited otherwise, like going to the drive-in movie theater. PG and I sat in the back seat while the couple, wanting to be alone, sat in the front seat sneaking embraces and kisses.

"I'm gonna tell Madear!" I sometimes cautioned them.

"You too nosy, boy," Jurdine would shoot back. "We ain't doing nothing."

"Y'all trying to kiss. I'm gonna tell it," I'd reply.

Of course, then John would move away from Jurdine and pretend to be interested in the movie. I never told Madear, though.

Everyone in the family liked John. He was a faithful church-goer, quiet, unassuming, and respectful. We were all happy when the engagement was announced.

Once we got word about the betrothal, Madear came alive. Now pregnant with Babebro, she got busy sending out invitations, making arrangements, preparing food.

The day of the wedding was chaotic. I never stopped running, doing an errand or a task.

"Lord, we don't have enough sugar for the punch. Brother, run to the store and get five pounds of sugar."

"Lord, the flowers ain't here yet! Brother, see what's keeping them flowers."

"Lord, Jurdine forgot to carry her shoes over to Miss Blow's. Brother, take them shoes 'cross the street."

By the time the wedding ceremony began, I was almost too exhausted to enjoy it.

But it was the wedding of the decade in Mansfield. Few people had seen one like it.

An early spring breeze kept the day cool as the wedding ceremony began. Daddy escorted Jurdine down the steps. The white wedding dress that a cousin had made was so long Jurdine had to be careful not to trip on the end of it.

People applauded when they saw her. She was beautiful! Nervously, Daddy braced himself to keep from stumbling. It seemed that all the Black people in Mansfield had come to the wedding.

There were so many people, I didn't get to see much of the ceremony. When I heard applause and cheering, I assumed Jurdine and John had said "I do."

Weeks later, people were still talking about the wedding.

"I ain't never seen a wedding like that."

"White folks couldn't of beat it."

Jurdine was so excited she couldn't stop talking about it, either.

"Sister looked good, didn't she, Brother?" she asked me.

"Yeah, Jurdine."

"A lot of folks were there, huh?"

"Yeah, a lot."

"I bet there won't be another wedding like it in a long time."

"No, I doubt it."

I missed my older sister after she and John moved into their own house. She had always looked after me and the other siblings. She had taught me how to dance and how to cook flapjacks.

A short while after the wedding, Madear's illness came back. Being pregnant with Babebro, the last of the Hudson children, made her condition even worse.

Now I was the oldest sibling in the house. More responsibilities fell to me. I learned how to cook while Madear was ill. She would call me to her bedside to give me directions for preparing a meal. Sometimes it was spaghetti and meatballs, or beans and rice or pork chops. I learned to fry chicken and how to cook white potatoes and collard greens. I even learned to make corn bread from scratch.

After Babebro was born, Madear's health began to improve. She had a medical procedure that prevented her from having any more children. Her body and her mind just needed time to heal from all the childbirths. She needed a period for a long exhale, a real deep breathing out so that the fresh air could replace the old.

Madear soon started work as a domestic for a White family to help bring in more money for our family. We didn't want her to, but the work gave her something to do outside of her own home and away from her family responsibilities.

CHAPTER 17

This Little Light of Mine

Every Wednesday at 6:30 p.m., adults and children alike gathered in our living room for Bible study. The weekly discussion had caught on in the neighborhood after Madear had initiated it. I remember when Madear first told me about her idea to start it.

"Some of these people round here don't know what it is to go to church," Madear told me on a cool fall day following my summer conversion. "They need to hear the word of God. We should have Bible study."

"You mean Bible study here at the house?" I asked curiously.

"Yeah! Why not? Ain't nothin' wrong with this house. We can have it right in this living room."

"But who's gonna teach it, Madear?"

"You can teach it."

"ME! I'm just twelve years old. I ain't no preacher!" I said.

"You don't have to be no preacher to talk about what's in the Bible," Madear replied.

Madear picked up a broom she had placed in the corner of the room and began sweeping the floor. Whenever she was done discussing something, when she knew her position would prevail, she moved on to something else. But I wasn't ready to agree. What did I know about the Bible? I read it sometimes. I listened intently to sermons, especially when Reverend Collins preached. But I wasn't an authority on the Bible. Me, leading Bible study? No way!

"Madear, I can't lead Bible study! I can't do it! You gotta get someone else to do it. Somebody who knows the Bible!" I protested.

Madear continued to sweep the floor although it wasn't necessary. She had swept it several times already. I expected her to burst into one of those hymns we used to hear her sing while she cooked, when her spirit needed soothing with the peace those hymns brought to her.

"Just let the Holy Spirit lead you, Brother. It ain't like you preaching or something. You just leading the Bible discussion, that all. Other folks will jump in to talk about what they read. You can do it. These people round here need to hear the word of God, especially these bad children. Just give it a try—you know Madear right."

"Aw, Madear! Shucks!"

It was over.

A week later, our first Bible study began. Madear had gotten the word out. Aunt Essie and her husband, Uncle OV, came. Two cousins, Annie Lee and Ella Mae, came. Our "adopted" brother Vida Blue was there. By 6:30, our living room was crowded.

I had selected a scripture, the Twenty-Third Psalm, days before. I read it over and over, trying to understand the complicated language of the King James Version Bible that was a staple in our home and in churches.

Madear opened with a hymn and everyone joined her in singing it. She also offered the prayer. I couldn't focus on it because I knew when she was finished, I was next. I was as nervous as I had ever been in my life. My legs shook and my hands trembled as Madear neared the end of her prayer. Long prayers were traditional in Mansfield, and I hoped Madear's would be the longest one ever. After she finished, I just stood there with the Bible in my hands, my eyes still closed, afraid to open them because of what I thought was a daunting task ahead of me.

"Brother," Madear called gently, bringing me to attention.

I opened my eyes and turned the pages of the Bible to the Twenty-Third Psalm. After clearing my throat, I began.

"Our . . . lesson . . . for today . . . is the . . . Twenty-Third Psalm . . . written by . . . David." My voice quivered as I struggled to get the words out.

"The shepherd boy, David. He killed Goliath!" someone shouted out.

The room erupted with laughter. I laughed, too. The laughter was a respite and it helped me to relax. I cleared my throat again.

"First, we're gonna take turns reading the verses, then we'll talk about what they mean. We'll start with you, Uncle OV."

So, our first Bible study was held right at our house on Mary Street, with me leading it. People shook my hand as they left.

"You did a good job, Brother," Uncle OV told me.

"Yeah, you led us real good," Cousin Ella Mae added. Madear just smiled all the while.

"See, you oughta listen to your Madear," she told me after everyone had gone. "Your mother know what she's talkin' 'bout."

After a year, PG and I alternated leading Bible study. Frank Milford, a preacher with aspirations of one day pastoring his own church, joined us and provided commentary and advice. Sometimes pastors in the area dropped by to offer their support. After I left to attend college, Bible study continued with PG leading it.

I was a serious Christian after I was baptized and became a member of Elizabeth Baptist Church Number Three. I tried to follow the precepts of the faith. Although I was barely a teenager, church leaders quickly began to give me responsibilities. I was asked to teach a Sunday school class. No meeting, activity, or event took place at the church without prayer. Sometimes I was called upon to offer it. Eventually, I was even chosen to lead the entire congregation in prayer during the regular church service. I often spoke before the church during special programs such as Youth Day. Sometimes I felt I wasn't ready to take on some of the responsibilities the elders suggested. But I held them all in such high regard, I never said no. When I stumbled or faltered, they picked me up and let me know it was all right.

Reverend Collins embraced me, encouraged me, and often told members how special he thought I was.

"Little Brother Hudson is gonna be a preacher one day," he would often say. I didn't think so, but I knew he meant it.

Less than a year after I joined church, Uncle Jamie died. He was just in his early sixties and his death caught everyone by surprise. I had grown close to him. He and Deacon Taylor were models of what a Christian man should be. My father was a good, caring man, but he was not a church man. If a church member was sick, Uncle Jamie came to visit and pray for them. So did Deacon Taylor. People sought their wisdom and welcomed their words of encouragement.

In Mansfield, as in many Black communities, Prince Hall Masons were special. Very few organizations held such a lofty status. Prince Hall Masons symbolized independence, authority, and self-reliance. The oldest and largest Black fraternity in the country was founded in 1784 by abolitionist leader Prince Hall in Boston. In 1850, an auxiliary, the Order of the Eastern Star, was established for women relatives of Masons. If you were a Mason or an Eastern Star, you were somebody, even if you didn't have the status others had in the community.

In 1951, Prince Hall Masons established a youth organization called the Order of the Knights of Pythagoras for boys eight to eighteen years of age. When a group was established in Mansfield, Bob Johnson kept his promise and offered me an invitation to join. I didn't really like the rituals and after several meetings, I decided not to return. Mr. Johnson didn't give up on me, though. When Masons in the northwestern part of the state gathered in Mansfield for a regional convention, he asked me and another student to address the body. I was thirteen.

"What should I talk about?" I asked Mr. Bob.

"That's up to you, young Hudson. I gave you the spot. You'll know what to do." Then he walked away.

But I didn't know what to talk about. Obviously, I had never been to a Masonic meeting. I wasn't a Mason. For several weeks I thought about what I should talk about. I asked my father for advice. He wasn't a Mason, but I thought maybe he would have some idea since some of his friends were "brothers."

"I don't know, son," was all he said. "Why don't you ask Bob? He should know."

"You know how Mr. Bob is, Daddy. I asked him and he just said I'll know what to talk about."

"Well, son, that's how he is. He always been that way. He must have thought highly of you if he asked you to speak."

I finally decided that I would talk about what a young Christian man should be. I drew from my own experiences, my own challenges. I didn't use profanity, although many of the boys in my peer group did. Some of them, when the opportunity was there, drank liquor. I enjoyed going to church while some of them didn't. Although the peer pressure to conform mounted, I resisted. So I decided to tell them that story. After writing the speech, I read it over and over and over and over until I felt I was ready.

That Saturday, the day of the convention, I sat dressed in my only black suit waiting for Mr. Bob to pick me up.

"I wish I could come, Bob," Madear told Mr. Bob when he got there. "I would love to be there to support my son."

"Well, you can't, Lurline. It's a Mason meeting and nobody but Masons can attend. I've been trying to get that husband of yours to join us. But he won't."

"You know my husband as well as I do, Bob," Madear said.

I got into the car and Mr. Bob pulled out of the driveway and sped off. When we arrived, I saw more Black men seated in that funeral home auditorium than I had ever seen in my life. There must have been several hundred of them. Mr. Bob escorted me to the stage, where the leaders of the various lodges were seated. As I sat there, staring out into a sea of Black faces, I looked down at the program someone had placed in my hand. My eyes focused on my name listed right in the middle of the other speakers.

I blanked. I was oblivious to everything happening around me. Speaker after speaker walked to the podium as the Masonic rituals continued. But I was unaware of all of them. I was in a daze. My mind started playing tricks on me. *You might mess up. Suppose you drop your speech on the floor? What if those men feel your speech is so terrible, they walk out on you?* I wanted to jump up from my seat and run out of the building. Why had I agreed to do it?

Suddenly, I thought I heard my name. I got up and walked

slowly to the podium, my speech in my hand. I looked out into the audience, but all those faces were one massive blur. I looked down at my paper and began the speech just as I had practiced it.

"Good character is a too often overlooked part of what it means to be a Christian," I told the men. "Men must be examples of what a good Christian is. But young men like me need men of character to be role models.

"I know Jesus Christ is the ultimate role model for us," I continued. "But having men that we see every day conducting themselves like sincere Christians is necessary, too. Young men need to know what forgiveness, grace, and mercy are so we can incorporate them into our lives. It makes it easier for us to learn their importance when we see older men employing them. I think that's why so many young men go astray. They don't see the right role models."

When I finished, I walked slowly back to my seat and sat down. I looked out into the audience again. All the men were standing, applauding vigorously. And for the first time in a long time, I saw faces again. Mr. Bob walked to the podium.

"We want to thank Brother Hudson for that powerful speech," he told his brothers. "Brothers," he added, "he issued a charge to us. Our future is in good hands."

The applause got louder. Finally, Mr. Bob called the convention to order and introduced the next speaker. As he made his way to the podium, I glanced at the program. When I located his name, it wasn't after mine. In fact, my name was farther down the list of speakers. I had gone to the podium and had spoken out of order.

"Oh, no," I said under my breath. My heart sank.

How stupid! I had been so nervous, so overwhelmed, I had lost all sense of time and place.

Feeling that I had been a total failure, for the remainder of the program I stared at the floor, embarrassed to look at the men who earlier had given my speech a rousing reception.

After the convention ended, I was ready to leave immediately. But the Masons wouldn't let me. They came to me, shaking my hand and embracing me.

On the way home, I apologized to Mr. Bob.

"I'm so sorry I spoke out of place," I told him.

"Don't worry about it, Hudson. You were tremendous."

"Yeah, but I spoke out of order."

"Don't worry about it, son. All the brothers really appreciated what you had to say. I'm gonna tell Wade to make sure he does everything he can to prepare you. One day, you're gonna be somebody important."

Mr. Bob encouraged me throughout my high school years, as did others in my small, rural town. The Christian values preached about, prayed about, talked about, and sung about at Elizabeth Baptist Church Number Three helped me appreciate the value of having meaningful relations—relationships based on mutual respect, understanding, and love for others.

But no one had more of an impact on my Christian growth than Madear. She volunteered me for programs at church.

Sometimes she would take me with her when she went to visit those who were sick. Once there, she was quick to ask me to pray for them.

"Brother, come go with me to see Ella Mae before it get too dark. She been sick in bed for nearly a week. I wanna take her something to eat."

"I was just getting ready to do some homework, Madear."

"It ain't gonna take long. I'm coming right back," she replied.

Of course, the visits always lasted a long time. Visits meant long, drawn-out conversations about topics that had been discussed many times before.

"You heard 'bout Bud?"

"Yeah, child. Poor thing. He got hisself in jail again."

I wondered, *Why are they talking about that again? Bud has been in jail for six months. They talked about it the last three times they got together.* It didn't matter. They were relatives sharing good conversation and connecting with each other.

Madear was an usher at church. It was a position she served in with pride. Many people sought her advice. Even those who some people thought were beyond redemption heeded her words of wisdom. One day she stopped a troubled young man in the neighborhood from attacking a teenager. Ray Brown had cornered a frightened youngster and was about to pound him with a bottle. Madear called to him to stop. After hesitating, Ray threw the bottle to the ground.

As Ray walked slowly away, Madear said softly to us, "That boy gonna get killed one day."

She was right. A few months later, Ray shot himself playing Russian roulette.

Very few people could have stopped Ray Brown that day. Madear did. Everyone respected her because they knew she cared and that she would do what she said. Many times, she called a shabbily dressed, hungry youngster into our house to give him or her a plate of food. She did it even during those times when she didn't have enough to feed her own children.

Daddy was a caring person, too. While growing up, there were times when I saw him get out of bed late at night to help someone who was in trouble. A handyman of sorts, he was called upon to help fix cars, make home repairs, even do yard work. Sometimes he took PG and me with him to lend a hand. He never said a word when one of Madear's siblings hit hard times and came to stay with us temporarily.

Daddy was a quiet man who relished being away from the limelight. He was in his world when he could sit with a cigar or cigarette, listening to a St. Louis Cardinals baseball game on radio or television or strumming his guitar with his eyes closed, perhaps visualizing being in another place. Madear, on the other hand, loved public engagement and prolonged conversations with almost anyone.

Both, however, demonstrated for all of us what sharing with others and caring about others looked like. They showed us in their interactions the value of respecting others, especially those who were facing difficult challenges. Daddy wasn't a regular churchgoer like Madear, but his life reflected many of the tenets of the Christian faith that even some regular churchgoers didn't adhere to.

"This Little Light of Mine" was one of Madear's favorite songs. When she sang it, you could swear that she thought she was onstage under beaming lights with thousands of eyes focused on her. She sang that song with passion, with feeling, with love.

This little light of mine,
I'm gonna let it shine.
This little light of mine,
I'm gonna let it shine.
This little light of mine,
I'm gonna let it shine,
Let it shine, let it shine, oh, let it shine.

Ev'rywhere I go,
I'm gonna let it shine.
Ev'rywhere I go,
I'm gonna let it shine.
Ev'rywhere I go,
I'm gonna let it shine,
Let it shine, let it shine, oh, let it shine.

Jesus gave it to me,
I'm gonna let it shine.
Jesus gave it to me,

I'm gonna let it shine.
Jesus gave it to me,
I'm gonna let it shine,
Let it shine, let it shine, oh, let it shine.

It was the theme song of the Hudson family, and our marching orders, too.

CHAPTER 18

A New DeSoto

For eighth grade I returned to DeSoto. It was not the same place I had left the school year before. Several new brick buildings now replaced the old wooden ones. A gym had been constructed, too, and new, more sturdily built bleachers had been added to the football field. Seventh and eighth grades were now junior high, and ninth through twelfth were high school grades. All elementary school students, grades one through six, were bused to Johnson Elementary. My one year as a junior high student went quickly.

The next school year, 1960, my first year as a high school student began. I was anxious and nervous because I really didn't know what to expect. I knew that, unlike in elementary school, students in high school changed classes every period and had more than one teacher. I knew there were more student activities. DeSoto had a reputation as a winner, a top institution in athletics and academics.

Our ninth-grade class was divided into groups, with roughly

thirty students in each. I was assigned to Group Three, the honors group. Some members of my group were classmates from elementary school, while others came from schools around the parish.

Our homeroom teacher, John Sherman Johnson, brought us all together in more ways than one. Mr. Johnson, who taught history, made us feel like a team rather than a class. Because we were considered the "bright" group, he pushed us. He didn't accept excuses, either. "Don't bring that lame answer in here," he would quickly tell a student who he felt was trying to find a way out of a challenge or a project. Many of us would remain together for four years.

At the beginning of the school year, I was hired to work in the school cafeteria. An hour before school started, I put cartons of milk into the large cooler so that they would be cold by lunchtime. After lining several large garbage cans with plastic bags, I put them in place so students could discard their trash. At the end of the school day, I helped the janitor move the filled cans to the back of the lunchroom so they could be carted away. I helped mop and sweep the lunchroom floor and helped to buff it when needed. I did this work for two years. PG replaced me during my junior year. For compensation, my siblings and I, all six of us, didn't have to pay for lunch, which for some families was a financial burden. I was proud to help my family.

My first year of high school was also the year of the presidential contest between Democrat John Fitzgerald Kennedy and Republican Richard Milhous Nixon. The campaigns dominated the news. On September 26, a few weeks after school began, the two candidates appeared in the nationally televised presidential debate. My father and I watched it.

I had begun to be more interested in issues that appeared on the news or in magazines I read. I had been aware of the Montgomery bus boycott in 1955–56 but was too young to appreciate its importance. I was just ten when nine Black students integrated Little Rock Central High School in 1957 and a division of the United States Army and the Arkansas National Guard, then under the control of the federal government, were called in to protect them from vengeful White segregationists. Initially, the Arkansas National Guard had been utilized to prevent the nine students from entering the school. By 1960, I had become more aware of the impact that national and local issues had on the world and on our town. There were passing references in the community about the civil rights movement, but discussions were rare. Most Black folks just worked hard and tried to avoid trouble that would bring them harm and put their family's lives and livelihood in jeopardy.

At school, teachers taught seriously and determinedly because they saw education as the lifeline to a better existence for their students and, consequently, for the community. But they had to be careful about what they said. The White school board, which had control over the education system, could fire teachers at will and had final approval over the school's curriculum. Those who were considered rebellious could be terminated in an instant.

But Black folks talked freely about the presidential election. White people permitted only a handful of Black people to vote because they believed they weren't a threat to them. But Black people talked about the coming election. John F. Kennedy was their choice. Richard Nixon supported maintaining states' rights, and Black folks knew what that meant: Racial discrimination and Jim Crow laws would continue unimpeded. So, they pulled for the Democratic nominee and hoped he would win.

"Kennedy got a lot to say," Daddy said as the camera pulled in for a close-up of the Massachusetts senator. "I don't trust that Nixon. He got a sneaky look."

"He wasn't a good vice president, was he, Daddy?"

"Not to me. Whatever little good that was done, Eisenhower did it. And that wasn't much."

"You think Kennedy will be good for Negroes?"

"Ain't none of 'em gonna be good for Negroes. Kennedy may do a little. In that way, he'll probably be better than Nixon. But we got to look out for ourselves," Daddy told me.

I watched the entire debate with my father. It was a rare occasion, because he rarely talked about politics, religion, or Black folks' issues with me. But when the conversation turned to baseball, he would talk literally nonstop.

"The Cardinals won again today. If they keep on winning, they just might do something. They oughta put George Crowe in there more. He got a hot bat."

A comment like that would start a long conversation about his favorite baseball team, the St. Louis Cardinals.

But I was becoming less passionate about baseball and sports. During my freshman year, I became a serious student. I started going to the school library to get books to read. I picked up magazines such as *The Saturday Evening Post, U.S. News & World Report, Newsweek, Jet,* and *Ebony* there, as well as at the homes of people who subscribed to them. The more I read, the more I wanted to learn about the world in which I lived and what had shaped it. What I learned made me more aware of what was happening around me.

Most Black folks in Mansfield were too busy or afraid to talk about the issues in which I had become interested. I was becoming more aware of racism, discrimination, and Jim Crow laws and their impact on Black people. I wanted to explore them, learn more about them, and do something about them.

The Mickey Mouse Club was a popular television show during the late 1950s. Produced by Walt Disney Productions, the variety show created for youngsters featured the Mouseketeers, a group of White teenagers who sang and danced. Black youngsters like me watched the show just as faithfully as White kids did. But there were no Mouseketeers who looked like us. That troubled me. It troubled me even more that it was so widely accepted that Black kids weren't allowed to participate.

I wondered where the Black kids were when I watched *American Bandstand,* a weekday show where White teenagers danced to the latest songs and recording stars performed their latest hits. It was that way on almost all the TV programs. No

Black people. So, I wrote a letter to Walt Disney Studios asking why there were no Negro Mouseketeers. The letter began politely, sharing how much I enjoyed the show. But I said I would enjoy it more if there were Negro Mouseketeers.

I got a response, but it didn't address the issue I raised in my letter. I was thanked for being a fan, and included in the envelope were several promotional posters that I threw away.

John F. Kennedy was elected president in November, becoming the first Catholic president. When he assumed office in 1961, he appointed his younger brother Robert as attorney general. I remember reading how Black people had helped the new president get elected. Catering to the Black vote had been a major strategy in Kennedy's campaign, and some said Robert was the architect. That prompted me to reach out to the attorney general when I decided to address racial conditions in Mansfield.

Robert Kennedy had been in office only a few months when I drafted a letter and sent it to him. In the letter, I told him about the plight of Negroes in Mansfield because of segregation and racism. Black people couldn't vote. White-only signs determined where we could go and what we could do. The good jobs went to White workers. Everywhere, Black people were prevented from exercising their rights as citizens.

I implored the new attorney general to do something about it. I didn't confer with anyone before writing the letter— not my parents, my siblings, or my teachers. I wanted to be solely responsible for my actions. I hoped I would get a positive response, but I didn't think I would. Why would someone as important as the attorney general of the United States take time from his busy schedule to answer a letter written to him by a Black boy from a small country town? *But at least, I thought, I can let him, or whoever reads the letter, know how I feel, that I care about what is happening to my people.*

After I mailed the letter, I started having second thoughts about sending it. What if it was misinterpreted and FBI agents were sent to our house? What if the letter was passed on to the White officials in Mansfield?

Some weeks later, I received a letter postmarked WASHINGTON, D.C. The return address was from the attorney general of the United States! In his letter, Attorney General Kennedy tried to assure me that the president and his administration were taking steps to address the unfair conditions Negroes faced. The letter was signed with his official signature.

I couldn't believe I had gotten an answer! I rushed to show my letter to Ma'am Ma. No one else would appreciate it the way she would. I knew what Madear would say: "Why you write to Washington like that? You just gonna make them White folks mad."

Daddy would express his dismay as well: "Son, what good will it do?"

Ma'am Ma saw it differently.

"What's this?" she asked me.

"The attorney general wrote to me," I answered proudly.

"The attorney general in Washington, D.C.?"

"Yes, ma'am."

"Lord, boy, what you into now?"

"I wrote him a letter about how Negroes are treated unfairly in Mansfield and he wrote me back. Read it, Ma'am Ma. Read it."

She took the envelope and slowly pulled the letter from it. I looked into her face, waiting to see the same excitement I had felt after I first read it. When she finished, she stared at it for a long time.

"Brother, you something else," she finally told me. I detected a hint of admiration. "What gave you the idea to write to the attorney general?"

"He's the one who told President Kennedy to reach out to Dr. Martin Luther King when he was arrested for protesting in Atlanta. He led the Negro strategy for his brother's presidential campaign."

"How do you know that?"

"I read it in magazines. I try to follow what's going on in the world," I told Ma'am Ma.

"You gonna be something special. Yes, you will. I just wish there was more Grandma could do to help ya," Ma'am Ma said.

She folded the letter and slid it into the envelope. Then she gave it back to me. I tried to hang on to it. First, I put it under my pillow, but it kept falling onto the floor. Then I placed it between the two mattresses on the bed. Months later when I looked for it, it wasn't there. I never saw it again.

In high school, I began to care even more about the plight of Black people and what was happening in the world. I was thirteen, nearly fourteen, a teenager and no longer a kid. I wanted to experience, to feel, to be with, to become immersed in what I was learning and not just repeat facts and information as I had done in elementary school.

History had always been my favorite subject—world history, American history, and even Louisiana history. I read intently the chapters about the Greeks and the Romans and the development of Western civilization. The founding of America, the growth of the country through what was called "manifest destiny," and the Civil War were subjects that commanded my rapt attention. The textbooks were really a homage to the greatness of the United States of America and Western civilization that White men had built. I plunged in, even as I tried to reconcile how my people were portrayed or, rather, left out. But in high school, I started to question what I was taught and what I wasn't taught.

In my ninth-grade English class, I wanted to learn more about writing. I paid particular attention to those sections of the textbook that featured poetry and excerpts from novels. I measured my writing against the poems in the textbooks. I read from poetry collections that were in the library, too. And I continued to write.

One day, Mrs. Gloria Collins, my civics teacher, approached me in the library.

"I see you're reading a magazine. Do you like keeping up with the news and current events?" she asked me.

"Yes, ma'am, I do."

"You know, every year some of our students participate in the district rally," she said. "The first- and second-place winners in each category go on to the state competition at Southern University in Baton Rouge."

I knew about the academic competition everyone called the rally. At DeSoto, academic accomplishments were lauded as much as successes in athletics. Every six-week marking period, the school held a convocation where all honor students were recognized. Students who won at the district and state rallies received special recognition, too. They were treated like superstars. We were encouraged to emulate them.

"Would you like to represent the school in the social studies category?" Mrs. Collins asked me. "The focus will be mostly on current events."

"Current events? You mean like what's going on now?"

"Basically, yes. I am the advisor for this category."

I looked at the magazine on the desk in front of me but didn't say anything.

Mrs. Collins placed a hand on her hip and stared at me. "Well?"

I looked up sheepishly. "I guess so."

Mrs. Collins began preparing me for the competition. She gave me magazines and clippings of important news stories. She invited me to her home, where she quizzed me on what I had read.

The Saturday the rally was held, teachers drove several carloads of students on a sixty-five-mile trip to Webster High School in Minden, Louisiana. It was the farthest I had ever been away from home.

I knew the answers to many of the questions. Some, however, were baffling. Who knew who the queen of the Netherlands was? And why was it important? I guessed Queen Juliana. When I returned home, I discovered I was correct.

A few days later, Mrs. Collins called me to her classroom.

"You won first place," she said, smiling. "Congratulations."

I tried to play it cool.

"I did?"

"Yes, you did. You will be going to Southern University in Baton Rouge to compete in the state competition."

My parents and siblings were more excited than I was when I told them I had won first place. During school assembly, all the first- and second-place winners were introduced to standing ovations. We were rock stars! Mr. Jacobs couldn't stop smiling as he sat on the stage looking more like a proud father than a school principal. Our success made the entire school proud.

Nearly two hundred miles away, the trip to the southern part of Louisiana would take four hours. Neighbors stopped by the house to give me money to help with expenses. They, too, let me know how proud they were of my accomplishment.

The morning of the trip, I placed the new clothes I had purchased in a small suitcase that I had been given for the trip. A large brown paper bag held fried chicken and slices of pineapple cake and sweet potato pie that Madear had prepared for me. When I left, she stood in the doorway holding open the screen door, something she had done countless times whenever one of her children left the house and would be away for more than a day.

Southern Louisiana looked so different from the northern part of the state. Northern Louisiana's rolling hills, forests, and farmland were replaced by bayous, swamps, and bridges. The trip took us across the Huey P. Long Bridge, and I marveled at the Mississippi River, which I had only read about in school. Soon, we were driving through an area where stores and other establishments lined the streets. I knew it was a Black community because I saw only Black people walking the streets.

"This must be the campus," I said excitedly after seeing a sign that read SOUTHERN UNIVERSITY DINER on one of the establishments.

"That's why we need to expose all of you to more than just what's in Mansfield," Joseph Jones, our chaperone, chastised me. "Because there is a sign that says 'Southern University' does not necessarily mean we're on the campus."

I felt small but recognized Mr. Jones was probably tired from the long drive he had done alone. After we crossed a railroad track, Mr. Jones told us we had now entered the campus.

As we drove down the main street leading to the center of the campus, I took in the sights, the buildings, so much land, so many students walking about briskly, as if they had somewhere to go. I was amazed.

This is like a city, I thought. *So this is what a college looks like.*

But what really caught my attention was the variety of colors of the students I saw.

"I thought Southern was a school for Negroes," I said to Mr. Jones. "I see White students, too."

Mr. Jones snapped at me. "Those aren't White students; they are Negroes, too. There is so much you all need to see, need to learn. Mansfield isn't the world. Negroes come in all colors. South Louisiana has a strong French influence. Many Negroes down here have French ancestry. They are called Creoles."

"We learned about that in our Louisiana history class in elementary school," one of the students added.

"Yeah, but they didn't have Negroes in that book," I corrected him. "At leas' I didn't see 'em in there."

"That's why it's important to go beyond the textbooks," Mr. Jones advised. "There is so much that textbooks don't cover."

The next day, we were ushered into a building where the competition was to be held. Rooms were filled with students. Every desk in the room I was sent to was occupied. None of us said much to each other. This test was much more difficult than the district one. Later, the first- and second-place winners were announced. Although I hadn't won, I felt I had done my best.

When we returned home, during assembly, the names of the students who had competed in the state competition were announced again and we received a standing ovation. We were all still treated like winners.

At home, I talked about my trip incessantly. My siblings and friends from the community peppered me with questions.

"What was south Louisiana like?" they wanted to know.

"You stayed in a dormitory? What was that like?"

"Some of the people speak Creole. What that sound like?"

The questions kept coming. I answered them all. I was one of the first in the neighborhood to have had such an experience.

CHAPTER 19

The Playwright

For several weeks, our tenth-grade American history class studied the differences between communism, which the textbook called "the evil threat to the United States," and democracy. One day, I mustered the courage to ask our teacher, Mr. Johnson, if I could write a play about communism and democracy that our class could perform.

"Why do you want to write a play?" he asked me.

"I think a play can help us better understand why democracy is different from communism," I answered.

"Have you written one before?"

"No, sir."

"Do you think you can write one?"

"I think I can."

"Write it and let me look at it," he said succinctly, and went back to grading papers.

But how would I write a play? I had never taken a course

in playwriting. I had read a few plays in our English text-books. A few times, teachers had organized skits for our classes to perform. But that's all the experience I had. Now I had to write a play about the differences between the two forms of government.

Why had I asked Mr. Johnson to let me write a play? I started second-guessing myself. How would I structure it? Who would the characters be? Then I remembered how much my father liked the legal TV drama *Perry Mason*. I enjoyed it, too, especially the tense scenes that unfolded in the court-room on every episode.

That's it! I said to myself. *I will put communism and democracy on trial in a courtroom.*

The next day, I went to the school library to get more information about the two forms of government. I also sought books that had plays in them so that I could learn more about the structure.

For the next two weeks, I stayed up late at night, reading library books and writing the play I titled *Communism versus Democracy*. In it, the prosecutor made the case for communism while the defense attorney represented democracy. Just as in *Perry Mason*, each called witnesses.

After delivering my play to Mr. Johnson, I couldn't sleep that night. What if he didn't like the play? What if he thought it was badly written? He certainly would let me know. Maybe I shouldn't have taken on a task that I might not have been prepared for.

I was unusually quiet the next school day. When I entered Mr. Johnson's class, I went directly to my desk.

"Hudson."

It was Mr. Johnson.

"Come here for a moment."

I walked slowly to his desk, dreading what he was going to tell me. He looked up at me.

"I read the play last night," he began in his no-nonsense manner, "and I think it's good. It's good. We should put it on."

I was stunned. I hadn't expected that answer. I wanted to shout I was so happy, but I managed to contain my excitement.

"We'll need somebody to direct it," I said, now turning to the staging of the play.

"That'll be you."

"Me?"

"Yeah, *you*. You wrote it. So you know better than anyone what to do with it."

"Thank you, Mr. Johnson."

As I turned to walk back to my desk, Mr. Johnson stopped me.

"Wade, you have a good grasp of what communism and democracy are. And it's all in the play. You did a good job."

I nodded. For the remainder of the school day, I was in a fog.

Our class performed the twenty-minute play. Students volunteered for the roles. I, of course, directed and played one of the attorneys.

I felt good about the performance, even if some of the

actors had to be reminded of their lines. Mr. Johnson's words of encouragement afterward meant a lot to me. As usual, they were delivered in his no-nonsense, forthright way.

"Wade, you keep on working," he told me. "There's a lot ahead of you."

CHAPTER 20

The End of Baseball

During the spring, my attention returned to baseball. For the first time in many years, DeSoto would have a high school baseball team. A few of us had approached Clarence Baldwin, the school's athletic director and head football coach, earlier in the school year about starting a team. Coach Baldwin agreed to add baseball for the spring semester and assigned one of his assistant football coaches, Mr. Rhodes, to coach us. We played smaller schools in the area, schools that Coach Baldwin sometimes called only a few days before to arrange for us to play a game. We didn't have uniforms, so we played in jeans and T-shirts. But we had a team.

Most of the members of the team came from our summer baseball program. We practiced every day after school. Coach Rhodes didn't know a lot about the rules, so he looked to us, especially me, for advice. We worked on turning the double play, stealing bases, hitting the cutoff man. We took batting practice.

We hadn't played but a few games when I awoke one morning with a terrible toothache. I tried home remedies, but they did little to ease the pain. Finally, with the left side of my face badly swollen, Madear took me to see a White dentist.

Just as there was no Black doctor, there was no Black dentist in Mansfield. The dentist told us the tooth had to be pulled. Madear trusted him, so she told him to pull it. The next morning when Madear came to check on me, I heard her gasp. I tried to ask her what was happening, but I could barely open my mouth.

"I gotta take you to the hospital. Get up and get dressed."

"What's wrong?" I finally was able to get out.

"I don't know. But something's wrong. Just get up and get dressed! Get up."

I was rushed to the hospital right away. Despite being dizzy and unable to comprehend what was going on, I could see a nurse and an attendant scurry about when they saw the left side of my face. Soon, I was submerged in a large tub of warm water, where I stayed for what seemed like hours. I fell asleep. When I awoke, I heard Madear ask a nurse, "Why the water turning that color, nurse?"

"That's the medicine working, auntie," I heard her answer.

I don't remember much about the first two days.

On the third day, as I lay in a bed in the Colored wing of the hospital, I asked Madear what had happened. She had been with me the entire time, sometimes sleeping in one of the chairs in my room.

"You had a bad tooth and it just got worse."

During my almost two-week stay in the hospital, class-mates came to visit. So did members of Elizabeth Number Three, including Reverend Collins. Even Mr. Jacobs, the school principal, paid me a visit to encourage me.

When I came home from the hospital, it seemed as if I had been away for months. When neighbors and family members came to visit, I sometimes overheard a few of them talking with my father and mother.

"Y'all should sue that dentist," Cousin Booth said. "He had no business pulling Brother's tooth like that if there was an infection."

"My child almost died," Madear responded. "I almost lost him. If I had waited a day or two longer, I probably would have."

"That's why you oughta sue him."

Others said the same thing.

But my father and mother were afraid.

"Lord, these White folks will run us out of town. Where would we go?" Madear said.

"I sued the company I worked for when I broke my leg. I had a few White folks on my side, but I didn't get hardly anything. Those folks almost blackballed me. I had a hard time finding another job. Thank God I got a good job at the funeral home now." Daddy's words said it all.

The day I went back to school, a game was scheduled for the baseball team. I was still weak and had lost some of the little weight on my tall, slender frame. When I was asked if I wanted to play, I answered yes quickly, grabbed a glove, and ran out to the second-base position. Early in the game the opposing team placed runners on first and second bases. The next batter hit a ground ball toward me. I charged it, thinking a double play would end the inning. As I moved forward, however, I stumbled. Seeing that the double play was no longer possible, I threw the ball to Cleonis at first base to retire the batter. Now runners were on second and third bases.

Suddenly, I heard Coach Rhodes yelling from the bench.

"What's wrong with you, Wade?! You had a double play. Why didn't you throw the ball to second?" I tried to ignore him, but he continued to yell.

"We could be out of the inning if you had thrown the ball to second base!"

"Could I have gotten the runner at second?" I asked Cleonis between pitches.

"I don't know. It would have been close," he answered.

When the next batter got a hit and the runners on base scored, Coach Rhodes began criticizing and scolding me again.

"You cost us two runs because you didn't make the play!"

I had finally had it.

"If you think someone else can play better, send them out here to take my place!"

And that's what he did. He sent Li'l Ray Woodley to replace me.

I slammed my glove on the ground and left the field.

"You probably came back to play too soon," Cleonis told me after the game was over. "Man, you been in the sickbed for two weeks."

During a game a few weeks later, Coach Rhodes called me over and asked me to explain a rule that had just had an impact on the game.

"The nerve of him!" I thought at first. "He's asking me for help after embarrassing me on the baseball field."

I did walk over to him. As I approached the coach, I could see the regret on his face. Maybe this was his way of apologizing.

Being away from the game had given me time to realize that my future was not in baseball. I was ready to move on from the game I had played since I was big enough to hold a bat and a glove. Leaving baseball freed me to focus on other things that were becoming more important to me—my writing and paying more attention to events occurring in the country.

CHAPTER 21

Awakening

What happened during 1963 was a revelation to me in so many ways and on so many levels. It was the year I began to question more profoundly what had been passed on to me culturally and in textbooks. Incidents of that year pushed me to ask questions. Finding answers to these questions inspired me to look at the world around me, at what was happening in the country, differently. This emerging new way of thinking had an impact on my classroom work. I began to lose interest in excelling academically. I didn't study as diligently as I once had.

So much happened during that one year, my junior year of high school. Much of it could be seen on the evening news on national television. I followed it as much as I could, sometimes watching NBC with Chet Huntley and David Brinkley and sometimes watching Walter Cronkite on CBS. When the national newscasts were expanded from fifteen minutes to thirty minutes in the fall of 1963, the new format allowed for much more news to be broadcast. We began to see more coverage of the civil rights movement in the South.

On January 14, during his inauguration as governor of Alabama, George Wallace declared "segregation today . . . segregation tomorrow . . . segregation forever."

These words stayed with me when I heard them. I knew he spoke for millions of White people, and for most of those who lived in Mansfield. What did that mean for my family, for all Black people? Did that mean there would be no end to the smothering grip that White superiority used to try to strangle us out of existence? What did it mean for me and my school friends who saw education as a way to lift ourselves? George Wallace and people like him had all the political and economic power, especially in the South. What were Black people like my family to do?

On May 3, I watched the news from Birmingham, Alabama. The day before, thousands had walked out of school to protest segregation. Theophilus Eugene "Bull" Connor, the city's commissioner of public safety, and the Birmingham police were determined to show who was in control. Television cameras and photographers captured the ugly violence that followed. The powerful force of fire hoses knocked students to the ground, and large, police-trained dogs attacked them, cornering them against buildings as they tried to get away.

As I watched what was happening to youngsters who looked like me, I got angry. I wished I was there. I wanted to be right there with the students, standing up for freedom, standing up against discrimination and racial bigotry. Yes,

I had written a letter to the attorney general of the United States about the treatment of Black people in Mansfield. I had written to Walt Disney Studios asking why there were no Black Mouseketeers. But those efforts paled when compared to what the students in Birmingham were doing. I grew even more angry when I heard a few Black people say things like "Those kids are being used" and "They oughta be in school. They just making things worse."

In fact, I had already heard some dissenting voices about the efforts of Dr. Martin Luther King Jr. I hadn't paid any attention to them at that time. But now it mattered.

I continued to watch every news broadcast to find out more about the students in Birmingham. I knew many of them had been arrested and a large number were expelled from school. But after a few days, the national interest in what became known as the Birmingham Children's Crusade waned. *Jet* and *Ebony* provided some information, but their magazine formats didn't allow them to cover it in depth. We never talked about it in class at school, and my parents never talked about it. Daddy watched the news coverage but said little. All Madear would say was "Lord, we have to pray. The devil sho' is busy."

So, I went into my own little world, writing down my thoughts and trying to find as much new information as possible with the limited resources that were available to me.

I sought refuge in the library. I went there often to read books, but found only a few about the Black experience— biographies of Booker T. Washington and George Washington

Carver. I read both. I read all the articles about the civil rights movement and about Black people that I could find in the magazines the library subscribed to. I was on a desperate search.

On June 12, the news of Medgar Evers's assassination broke. I watched the coverage on the evening news the next day. I saw the driveway where he had fallen when he was slain. I saw the distraught faces of his wife, Myrlie Evers, and their children. I was angry. No, I was furious! Why did these bad, violent things continue to happen to Black people?! Medgar Evers was only trying to help Black people in Mississippi secure the right to vote and have access to good jobs.

As with the Children's Crusade in Birmingham, the news media soon moved on. But I couldn't move on. I kept thinking about Medgar Evers giving his life for what those in the civil rights movement called "freedom." I thought about the unfair treatment Black folks in Mansfield tolerated.

All of this was on my mind when I picked up a copy of *Playboy* magazine that I had purchased some months before. I kept it hidden underneath the mattress of my bed so no one else would see it. When I opened the pages to thumb to the centerfold again, an interview with Malcolm X conducted by Alex Haley caught my attention. I had missed it before. I didn't know much about the fiery spokesman for the Nation of Islam, the members of which most people referred to as Black Muslims. Many people associated Malcolm X's name with hatred and violence. Many Black people in Mansfield were leery of him because they believed he was anti-Christian and advocated for a race war. That frightened them.

At first, I wasn't going to read the interview. But I saw a pull quote that read:

> "Christ wasn't White. Christ was a Black man.
> Only the poor, brainwashed American Negro has
> been made to believe that Christ was White, to
> maneuver him into worshipping the White man."

It caught my attention.

What! Christ wasn't White? He was Black!

I was startled. I stared at that quote, trying to make sense of it. I had never considered Christ being anything else but White. All the pictures I had ever seen showed him as a White man with long straight blond hair flowing over his shoulders. That included the pictures of him in our own home. Black? Could he have been Black?

Now the interview had my attention. It was long, but I read all of it. Toward the middle of it, Malcolm said:

> "After becoming a Muslim in prison, I read almost
> everything I could put my hands on in the prison
> library. I began to think back on everything I had
> read and especially with the histories, I realized
> that nearly all of them read by the general public
> have been made into white histories."

When Alex Haley asked Malcolm to name a few, the Black leader cited names, lands, and people I had never heard of before or that I hadn't known were considered Black. Malcolm talked a lot about his Muslim faith. I was a committed Christian, so I didn't relate to that. But what Malcolm said about the way history had been written to create a White version, leaving out and devaluing what Black people had contributed, resonated with me. I had never heard this perspective, a perspective where Black people were at the center. I reread those sections. It all made sense to me. It also meant I had a lot to learn. And unlearn.

I talked with PG about what I had read. But hardly anyone else was interested. The media had done a successful job of making Malcolm into someone to be shunned and rejected because he was a "madman" associated with a dangerous cult. Whenever I could find a story or an article about Malcolm, I read it. There weren't that many. I often wished I was living in Harlem so I could hear and learn from him directly.

Toward the end of the summer, teachers and students started preparing for another school year, my senior year. The news media began covering an upcoming march in Washington, D.C., by civil rights advocates. Scheduled to take place on August 28, the March on Washington for Jobs and Freedom was expected to draw people from across the country, Black and White, young people and adults, men and women, labor and religious leaders. Some news journalists said it would be the largest rally in the history of the United States.

Very little was said about this historic event in Mansfield.

At least I didn't hear much about it. On the day of the march, Roger Mudd covered it live for CBS News. March organizers expected one hundred thousand people to attend, but more than two hundred thousand assembled in the nation's capital. Contrary to what authorities and those who were against the march had speculated, there was no violence.

I wanted to be in Washington, D.C. I wanted to march, too, with my poster, singing freedom songs just like all the thousands of other young people I saw on television. I wanted to hear the important speeches and listen to popular recording stars perform. But, most of all, I just wanted to be there, to be in that number, to be counted when it mattered. I felt hurt, deflated, that I wasn't there.

That evening, the national networks interrupted their regular programing to show scenes from and to comment on the march. I was moved when I heard parts of Dr. Martin Luther King Jr.'s "I Have a Dream" speech. When he said that one hundred years after the signing of the Emancipation Proclamation, Black people were still not free, I stood up and applauded. Then he said Blacks were still crippled by the manacles of segregation and the chains of discrimination. I recognized that plight in Mansfield.

"Do you think something might change?" I asked Daddy that evening.

"I hope so, son. It certainly can't git no worse."

"I wish I could of been there," I lamented sadly.

"Well, it takes a lot of money to go to Washington, D.C.," Daddy replied.

"They said on the news that a lot of people came on buses. I wish someone here could of gotten a bus. I sho' would have gone."

Daddy looked away.

"I'm sure there will be plenty of other opportunities," he said. "It gonna take a lot to change things."

When school started a few weeks later, I expected that we would talk about the march in one of our classes. But we never did. It made me even more determined to be a fighter for freedom.

In my heart I already was. Sometimes I would lie awake at night, visualizing myself in some of the places where the struggle was being waged. Like so many others, I, too, imagined myself being arrested for marching, for picketing, for sitting in. Handcuffed, I, too, was thrown in jail with other freedom fighters, where we sang freedom songs such as "Ain't Gonna Let Nobody Turn Me 'Round," "We Shall Overcome," and "Oh, Freedom." Yes, I was on the battlefield, stepping up to change things so my people could know what it felt like to be free.

The more I followed the civil rights movement, the more I lost interest in school. I did enough to remain an honors student, but I was no longer driven to excel.

On September 15, I rose early to get ready to go to church. It was a third Sunday, a special Sunday of the month for us at Elizabeth Baptist Church Number Three. I was thinking about a lot of things that morning. I had to select a college that I would attend. Although I really wanted to go and join the civil rights movement, I knew attending college was what I had to do. Everyone expected me to go. I was a top student. We were told education was a key to success. So, I had started thinking about college seriously. What school should I select? Would I have enough money for it? Since I had to go to college, I decided that I would attend one out of state, far away from Louisiana.

After returning home from another spirited church service, I learned the shocking news out of Birmingham. In the ladies' room in the basement of the 16th Street Baptist Church, five young Black girls had been chatting about the first days of school and their participation in the Youth Day morning service. Suddenly, a bomb exploded under the front steps of the church, killing four of the girls, fourteen-year-olds Addie Mae Collins, Cynthia Wesley, and Carole Robertson, and eleven-year-old Denise McNair. Addie's sister Sarah survived, but she lost an eye in the bombing. The bomb had been planted by members of a local chapter of the violent racist group the Ku Klux Klan.

When I heard the news, I was stunned. I didn't know what those girls looked like, but I saw faces that could be theirs flashing before me. They could have been some of the girls who were at church with me earlier. They could have been some of my classmates. They could have been some of my brothers or my sister. They were just a few years younger than me. *How could anyone be so mean and hateful?* I thought. But I already knew the answer.

When I finally went inside the house, I could hear Madear

singing one of her gospel songs to find some consolation as she prepared dinner. Daddy didn't seem too interested in the baseball game.

I thought about my siblings, PG, Lillo, Curtis, Lauriece, Jurdine, Raymond, and Babebro. What would I do if racist White Ku Klux Klansmen murdered one of them?

It was a difficult day for me. I wanted to do something, but I felt helpless.

At school the next day, students talked about the terrible event. It took a while for me to get my bearings again. But each time an incident like what happened at 16th Street Baptist Church occurred, the more conscious I became. I wanted to be an activist, a civil rights worker.

A couple of months later, I sat in English class. Lunch had just ended and all the students in class were trying to get back into the flow of classroom work. At least most of us. It was a Friday, though, and a long week of school was about to end. Most students were thinking about the coming weekend and making plans for the two-day respite. It would soon turn cold, so on Saturday I planned to go downtown to purchase a winter coat. Suddenly, Charles Johnson, the star basketball player at school, yelled out "The president's been shot." He frequently listened to a transistor radio while he sat in the corner of the room, where it was difficult for our teacher, Miss Henderson, to see him.

"Stop playing round," someone told him. "You always joking."

"Charles, what are you doing with that radio in class,

anyway?" Miss Henderson asked pointedly. Like Mr. Johnson, Miss Henderson didn't play. All the students knew she was all business.

"I'm not playing, y'all!" Charles insisted. "President Kennedy been shot in Dallas. He was riding in a motorcade."

Charles turned up the volume on the radio and we all heard the news that was making its way across the country and around the world. We sat in stunned silence, not believing what we were hearing. But it was real. During those days, if it was on the news, it was real.

"Why would somebody kill the president?" someone wondered out loud.

"Y'all heard 'bout the president gittin' shot?" a student asked, poking his head into the room.

Our lack of a response provided the answer. The student shook his head and closed the door quietly as he left.

The three national networks, NBC, CBS, and ABC, presented nonstop coverage as people everywhere watched. It seemed as if people all around the country were in mourning. Then, on that Sunday, Lee Harvey Oswald, the man who had been apprehended and accused of the assassination, was killed. Cameras rolled as police and press converged in the basement of the Dallas Police Headquarters, where Jack Ruby shot Oswald, the alleged assassin. In just two days, one event had shaken the nation to its core, and another sent it reeling even further.

"What's happening to our world?" people were asking.

Earlier in the year, on June 11, on national television,

President Kennedy had proposed legislation to address civil rights in the country. Some people, especially Black people, believed he was killed because of that. Even some Black folks in Mansfield whispered it in the privacy of their homes. Whatever the reason, the president had been killed and violence had wreaked havoc in the country, especially against Black people as the push to end racial discriminatory laws and customs intensified.

My awakening opened my eyes in so many other ways and sensitized me to the plight and struggles of others in society, too. So, I continued to question. I persisted in trying to find answers to those questions. For example, why was girls' basketball so different from the game that boys played?

Basketball was the only sport that girls could play at DeSoto. Six players were on the court instead of five as in the boys' game. Three forwards played offense and three guards were on defense. Only the forwards could shoot the ball, and they had to remain in their team's frontcourt. Guards had to remain in the backcourt. Once in possession of the ball, players could only dribble several times, after which they had to pass or shoot. I had never really thought about it before. I had just accepted that it was different. But now I wanted to know why.

The next day, I went to the school library to find a book that would explain why the girls' basketball game was so different from the boys'. I already knew much of what I discovered but hadn't thought much about. Women were portrayed as the weaker sex, as not being as strong as men. Those books claimed that girls were too frail to play basketball the way boys could. They didn't have the strength, the stamina, or the dexterity. So, the game had to be altered, watered down to compensate for their weaknesses.

Many schools believed that girls shouldn't play competitive sports at all, including basketball, so girls' sports weren't offered. Girls were supposed to learn how to take care of the home and raise children. Boys, on the other hand, should learn how to be rough and tough because that prepared them for their roles as leaders of organizations and businesses and to fight wars as soldiers. Movies, books, and institutions such as schools and even churches reinforced this view of gender roles in society.

Popular television shows that we watched, such as *Leave It to Beaver, Father Knows Best, The Adventures of Ozzie and Harriet,* and *The Donna Reed Show,* presented families where the father was the sole authority. The mother was a housewife who was happy to spend each day cleaning, preparing meals, taking care of the children, and making the home comfortable for the husband when he returned home from a long workday. These television programs devalued women. Boys like me saw the men as role models, always in charge, always running things. Television stars were almost all men. Few women were doctors, lawyers, judges.

Even in my church, men prayed the important prayers and were the church leaders. In churches, women were prohibited from becoming ministers or even standing behind the pulpit. Very few of them held elected office in local, state, and federal governments.

Nearly every aspect of society declared directly and profoundly that it was a man's world. And that determined how I and other boys related to the girls and women in our lives. Most of us assumed our lofty positions as superior when in so many situations we were inferior. Aggressive boys felt emboldened to touch girls inappropriately, to call them disparaging names and use sexist terms blatantly in front of them and to them. In elementary school and in high school, it was a game for boys to grab a girl's behind and laugh about it. Sometimes teachers punished the boys when a girl fought back or complained, but that never stopped them. Boys felt entitled and girls were often helpless and could do no more than slap their hands away.

President Kennedy had signed the Equal Pay Act on June 10, 1963. The new law was aimed at abolishing wage disparity based on sex. I had never thought about what women were paid compared to men. I knew Black people, men and women, were paid far less than White people. But that was it.

I began to understand that the way women and girls were treated was unfair. And I realized that I had to grow and had a lot to learn myself. I had discovered the Malcolm X interview while perusing a magazine that marginalized women.

When I watched those cowboy movies I enjoyed so much, I never thought about the terrible treatment Indigenous people, called "Indians," received. In the 1950s and 1960s, television was inundated with shows like *Gunsmoke, Bonanza, Cheyenne, Maverick, Wagon Train,* and *Rawhide.* They showcased the shootouts, the good cowboys chasing the bad guys on horseback, the fastest-draw contests. The action was gripping and kept my rapt attention. My interest peaked when Indigenous Americans were the villains. I pulled for the U.S. Cavalry when Indians attacked their forts or when they attacked wagon trains headed west. My friends and I cheered as the cavalry came to the rescue of White settlers who were about to be annihilated by the marauding Cherokee or Kiowa.

The plot buildup to the rescue was palpable. Indians scalping helpless White settlers and the partner of the White star of the movie screaming "You dirty savages!" helped to set the stage for the heroic rescue. So, when it came, jubilation was inevitable. As the Indians succumbed to the superior weapons of the U.S. Army, we joined the rescued White settlers in yelling for the Indians' total demise. Repeatedly, these themes were drilled into our consciousness.

There were no counternarratives to them. So, we grew up bombarded by these TV shows, movies, and books, encouraged to believe that Indigenous people and other people of color from Japan and China and those who came from different cultures were not "Americans," were not "one of us."

Every so often, however, a movie or TV show portrayed these "non-Americans" in a sympathetic light. The White star came to the rescue, confronting the irate, obviously racist ringleader. Never were systemic racism and discrimination addressed. The problem was always the few who didn't represent America's true ideals and values. Seldom were Black people and other people of color portrayed as having power. Often, they were helpless and sympathetic characters.

I began to unfurl the carefully made blanket of racism and discrimination, sexism, intolerance, and indifference with which I had been covered.

I recognized that I knew little about the history of Black people and that there was so much more I had to learn. Now I wanted to know about those excluded histories, about those people that the history we studied had marginalized and neglected.

But where was I to go? Our teachers were not free to cover this history even if they wanted to. Most were not prepared because they had been taught in the same European tradition. So I became frustrated. The more the civil rights movement played out on television news and in newspapers and magazines, the more I wanted to know. My interest in the classes I was being taught continued to decline.

I was developing a yearning that I didn't quite understand. More and more, I began to think beyond Mansfield, wondering what it would be like if I lived in Harlem or some other place where my yearning could be addressed, where my desire to know more could be fed. Still, I had a final year of high school to complete, a graduation to attend, and a college to select.

CHAPTER 22

Last Year

The DeSoto High School class of 1964 listened to "Heat Wave" by Martha and the Vandellas, "It's All Right" by the Impressions, "Cry Baby" by Garnet Mimms and The Enchanters, "The Way You Do the Things You Do" by the Temptations, and "Walking the Dog" by Rufus Thomas. We boogied when they were played on record players at house parties that a few parents allowed their teenagers to throw.

I had already begun my search for the institution I wanted to attend. I sent for catalogs from different colleges and universities around the country and read them all thoroughly, trying to determine if I would feel at home at one of them. I examined every photo of campus life to find at least one Black student. I threw away those catalogs that didn't include us. Those that did, I placed in my "to keep" pile. They were in the western and northern parts of the country and included schools like the University of California Los Angeles, the University of Southern California, the University of San

Francisco, the University of Michigan, Michigan State University, and New York University.

Many colleges and universities in the country didn't accept Black students. Some that accepted Black students didn't really want them on their campuses. In the South, however, there was no question. Black students were not allowed to attend those colleges and universities.

People around me, at church and at school, always assumed I was going to college. My parents wanted me to go. Teachers encouraged me to attend. I would be the first in my family to do so, and I knew no one in my extended family who had gone. Even neighbors expected that I would go to college.

But a part of me really wanted to join the civil rights movement, maybe hook up with John Lewis and the Student Nonviolent Coordinating Committee or with Dr. Martin Luther King Jr. and the Southern Christian Leadership Conference in the fight for freedom. That's where my heart was. That's where I felt I was needed. I wanted to make a difference, to make life better for those around me, to help to end discrimination and prejudice. But for my family and those in Mansfield who loved and cared about me, there was no other option but going to college.

Madear had already talked to school administrators about my coming back to teach at one of the schools in DeSoto Parish after I had gotten my degree. Just as she always took charge of everything else in her sphere of influence, she was trying to take charge of my career.

"Brother, you can come back here and teach." She tried to sound convincing. "You can have a job waitin' on ya when you finish college."

"I don't wanna come back here to teach, Madear. You trying to plan my future for me. You trying to control my destiny."

"Your what?"

"My destiny."

"I don't know what you talkin' 'bout. You don't wanna come back here? What's wrong with stayin' here? Your family is here. All of your friends is here."

"That doesn't mean I have to stay here, Madear. I gotta find my own destiny."

"What's wrong with ya, boy? What you talkin' 'bout? You actin' crazy."

"Madear, I wanna make a difference. I wanna do something important like Martin Luther King is doing."

"You mean going to jail? What's that doing? Who's that helpin'?"

"Dr. King trying to change things, Madear. Sometimes that means you might have to go to jail or even get beat up or arrested."

"You can change things right here. Look at what Mr. and Mrs. Blow is doing. You can be just like them."

"I respect them, Madear, but I have to find what's best for me."

"You too young to figure out what's best for you."

"You just want me to stay 'round here with y'all. You just don't want me to leave."

"What's wrong with that? You my child!"

Always reluctant to relent during a discussion or an argument, Madear turned away and looked for something else as a distraction. Was one of those gospel songs coming?

"I don't understand you. Maybe Wade can talk some sense into you." Then she walked away.

But all Daddy would say was "Lurline, let the boy do what he wanna do. It's his life."

Madear never gave up. She continued to push me to accept her plan for me throughout my senior year.

If I had to go to college, it wouldn't be one in the South. That's what I had determined. So, I continued to look at out-of-state institutions. That is, until I had a conversation with one of my best friends at school. Bobby Gilliard and I had struck up a friendship during our freshman year. We both followed sports closely and enjoyed talking about what was happening in the world. Like me, Bobby was considering out-of-state colleges.

"Did you see how much it cost to go to Ohio State?" he asked me one day. "It cost a *loooot* of money."

"Yeah, I've been looking at the tuition at a lot of these schools. The out-of-state fee is a killer."

"Then it costs money to travel to get to them," Bobby said. "I don't know."

"Me, either. I was getting ready to send my application to USC until I saw how much it cost. We don't know anybody that can help us try to get a scholarship."

"You have to be good in sports to get a scholarship. That ain't us."

Bobby was a relief pitcher on the baseball team, but neither he nor I was good enough to be offered an athletic scholarship. So we started looking at institutions in the state.

I looked at catalogs from Grambling College in the northern part of the state and Southern University, the only state-supported Black institutions. Private Black colleges included Dillard and Xavier Universities in New Orleans, but they were more expensive than state-supported institutions.

Some of my classmates were planning to go to Grambling or Southern. Mr. and Mrs. Blow had attended Wiley College, a Black college in Marshall, Texas. Both encouraged me to consider going there. Some teachers pushed Grambling while others thought Southern University offered more opportunities for me. I thought Grambling, only an hour-and-a-half drive, was too close to home. I could close my eyes and see Madear walk into my dormitory room with a plate of food.

So I applied to Southern University, much farther away. Since I was going to college, I decided I would become a lawyer and not a teacher. As a lawyer like Thurgood Marshall, who had won many landmark civil rights cases, I could be a better asset to the civil rights movement. Although I had continued to write throughout high school, I never considered pursuing writing as a career. Since I didn't know any Black writers, I didn't think there was a future in it for me.

I applied for scholarships with the help of several teachers. Mr. Blow and Reverend Collins wrote letters of recommendation for me. Then, I waited for a response from the university.

I tried to enjoy my last year as best I could. I was a member of the Honor Society. Bobby and I, along with another classmate, Carrie Abraham, represented the school in a drama competition that drew schools from around the region. We rehearsed nearly every day for weeks and I spent a lot of time at home learning my lines. Acting helped with my writing. Before, when I wrote a poem or an essay, I read it silently. But reciting lines from the play helped me realize that hearing words spoken out loud and performed could unleash their power. It also allowed me to understand what words, what lines, what sentences, what paragraphs, worked or didn't work.

During the second semester, in early 1964, a young Black fighter caught my attention. Cassius Clay was brash, self-assured, and unafraid. He spoke his mind, even when interviewed on television. I had never seen a Black person like him before. Any Black person who had the fortunate opportunity to achieve a degree of success or to open a door that had been closed to other Black people was expected to be humble and grateful and to conduct himself or herself in a "dignified manner." Not Cassius Clay.

Daddy loved boxing as much as he did baseball. He watched every fight that was televised. His favorites were Joe Louis when he was still active, Archie Moore, and Sugar Ray

Robinson. All three spoke little when interviewed and were willing to remain in their designated places. My father saw them as the right models for Black people. He didn't think much of Cassius Clay.

"Clay is such a bigmouth," he often said. "Somebody gonna shut him up."

But we youngsters thought he was cool. Maybe he did boast a little too much. But he had flair and style. And he didn't take stuff off the White folks.

When the heavyweight championship bout between Cassius and titleholder Sonny Liston was announced for February 1964, most people thought the braggadocious young fighter would finally be shut up for good. Even my father thought that, and hoped for it. But by the date of the fight, I had become a Cassius Clay fan. Although my father wasn't a fan of Sonny Liston because he had knocked out Floyd Patterson twice, he chose him over Clay. When Clay won and "shocked the world," as he described it, I kept my excitement under wraps because Daddy wasn't at all pleased by the result.

But most of the guys at school were excited. We all embraced the new champion's boast in the ring after he had won. "I'm a bad man!" he yelled. "I'm a bad man!" We felt "bad," too . . . like "bad" young Black men. Very few people had given Cassius Clay a chance and almost all White people had pulled against him. But he had defied the odds. So we walked around with our heads held high, believing we could defy the odds, too.

Later, when I heard that Sam Cooke, Malcolm X, Jim

Brown, and Cassius had partied together after the fight, I got even more excited. Sam Cooke was my favorite singer. Jim Brown was my favorite football player. Malcolm X had helped fuel my desire to learn more about my history. A few months later, Cassius Clay became a Muslim and was given the name Muhammad Ali.

CHAPTER 23

Graduation

As spring moved on, we began preparing for graduation ceremonies, and the Hudson family was excited. Most of my siblings were old enough to comprehend what my graduation meant. PG was now sixteen; Lillo, thirteen; Curtis, eleven; Lauriece, nine; and Raymond, eight; and Babebro would be five years old in July. I had watched them as they grew up. I had looked after them. Sometimes, as the oldest brother, I had chastised them. They often came to me for advice.

We were a close family. They all were happy for me to reach a milestone that no one else in the family had. Madear let everyone she talked with know that her son would soon be graduating. So did Ma'am Ma. Papa didn't like to brag, but he too shared the good news. My neighbors, members of my church—all were proud of me.

Daddy was happy that I was about to graduate. But he didn't express it. Since Bob Johnson had given him a job at the funeral home, that's where he was most of the time. For the last few years of high school, he often wasn't home. He always said he had a lot of work to do. So we all thought that that was the reason he didn't come home.

It never occurred to me that perhaps my parents' relationship was not the same as it had been. Madear complained about Daddy being away from home so much, but I thought she was exaggerating. We had always been one big family . . . if not always happy, always together, caring for each other. It felt odd sharing news with Daddy at the funeral home where he worked, and not at home. But I just accepted it.

One day I asked him why he didn't come home much since he had started working at the funeral home.

"Madear say you've abandoned the family," I told him.

"No, son! I haven't abandoned y'all or Lurline," he responded. "Don't listen to your mama."

"But why don't you come home more?"

"Son, I'm just working hard."

He pulled out a cigarette and lit it.

"I got a lot of responsibilities here at the funeral home. I got work that's piled up back there now."

"You sure, Daddy?"

"Son, you know your daddy wouldn't lie to you."

I dropped it.

Madear was a constant in the family. No matter what her children faced, she was there, trying to mitigate their pain, and always sharing their joys, their accomplishments, their failures. Whenever any of us called on her we knew she would, as the old folks in Mansfield used to say, "walk through hell and high water to get to us." She was Madear!

Graduation week came quickly. When we got our caps and gowns, we all knew that graduation was real. I didn't like the way the cap sat atop my head, but I had to wear it.

But before graduation ceremonies, there was prom night. Many of the guys didn't take dates. We came looking to have fun and find a date at the event. And did we party. Alcohol wasn't allowed, but of course that didn't stop the fellows from bringing it.

I was seventeen years old and I had never had an alcoholic drink in my life. My parents forbade drinking. Although I had had opportunities to do so, I refused to, even being willing to withstand my friends' teasing and ridicule. But I got caught up in the excitement of prom evening. When Robert Murray, whom I had known since childhood, offered me a drink from a bottle of whiskey, I took it. The bottle was passed around, but it found me more than the other boys.

It was a setup and I didn't recognize it. It didn't take long for me to become inebriated. Seeing that I was about to pass out, Rob brought me home and carried me from the car to the front door.

"Rob, what's wrong with my son?" I heard Madear ask after she opened the door.

"I think he had a little too much to drink, Miss Leen," Rob answered, half laughing.

"Rob, you know Brother ain't used to drinking like y'all is."

"He'll be all right."

Rob kept smiling. As he stood there holding me up, I am sure his glee was sparked because he had succeeded in getting me drunk. I was someone he saw as a straight arrow.

I awoke the next morning, vowing to never take a drink of alcohol again in my life.

Most days in late May were hot and were a taste of hotter weather to come. I knew graduation was going to be a hot day.

"Brother, you got everything together? They want ya there early."

"Yeah, I got everything, Madear."

Every Hudson child stared at me as I buttoned the coat to my black suit. They all wanted to go to see their oldest brother graduate.

"I don't think there's anything wrong with them going, Madear."

"Them children don't need to go. Let 'em stay here. They'll just git in the way."

Shrugging one shoulder toward my siblings, I said, "I tried."

Then I was on my way, making the same walk I had made for years.

"I'll get your daddy there on time," Madear yelled to me as I walked briskly out of the yard and up the street.

As I passed, people noticed me in my black suit. They all knew it was the day of high school graduation.

"Congratulations, Brother!" someone shouted as I passed.

"We proud of you!" another said.

"I know Lurline and Wade proud of you!" uttered another.

These east-side folks were proud of me, too. They were proud of all the graduates. High school graduation wasn't just a school event, it was a ceremony for all Black people in town.

"You graduating today?" a little girl asked as I hurried past. She stopped jumping rope for a moment to hear my reply.

"Yep. I sure am."

"I'm gonna graduate, too!" she declared, and went back to jumping rope.

Classmates, gathered in clusters, greeted me when I arrived at the gym, which had been set up for the ceremony.

We had already rehearsed how to march in, where we would sit, and how we would walk to the stage to receive our diplomas. Extend the right hand for Principal Jacobs and other school officials to shake and accept the diploma with the left. Don't talk. No gum chewing.

By the time we had all donned our graduation regalia and taken our seats, the gym was crowded. The hot late-spring weather caused most of us to perspire as we waited for the speeches to end and our names to be called.

Finally, my turn came. I walked to the stage determinedly, each step measured and sure. After receiving my diploma, on my way back to my seat, I took a quick look at Madear and Daddy, seated in the audience. Madear had a big smile on her face. Even the normally unanimated face of my father had a smile that had sneaked up and stayed for a while.

When I sat back in my seat, I looked around at the students

who surrounded me. Of the 212 who had entered high school four years earlier, 134 had made it. We were the largest graduating class in the history of the school.

When the ceremony ended, parents and friends descended upon us.

"I'm so proud of you, Brother," Madear told me, looking directly into my eyes. Then she gave me a big hug.

"I'm proud of you, too, son," Daddy added. He reached for my hand and shook it.

I had done it! I had graduated from DeSoto High School! Before receiving my diploma, I'd thought it wouldn't be a big deal. It would be just another step in the process. But holding that diploma in my hand felt special. I was an honors student, finishing in the top 10 percent of my class. I was a member of the Honor Society and had received several scholarships.

As I stood with my parents, receiving congratulations from students, teachers, and other parents, I wondered if I should have been more studious during my last year. Maybe I could have finished higher in my class and perhaps could have gotten more scholarship offers. But I had no regrets. I had begun the first steps of a journey that could lead to a better version of who I was meant to be, what I had to learn and achieve. My future would be shaped by new experiences that awaited me. My hunger to learn more would be fed by them. It was a journey that I was eager to take.

Daddy dropped Madear and me off at home. I was mobbed when I walked into the house.

Later, extended family dropped by to congratulate me.

Neighbors came over. Some of the Mary Street Boys, too. But Aunt Margaret remained her feisty self.

"Lurline, y'all going crazy over that boy."

"You proud of him, too, Margaret." Madear placed her right hand on her hip defiantly. "Ya just jealous, that's all."

My younger aunt spun around and started for the door.

"Child, y'all something else."

We all laughed.

I know she was proud, too. But she was too stubborn to show it.

CHAPTER 24

Goodbyes

All summer I prepared for my first year at Southern University. I read about the university's history. How P.B.S. Pinchback, the first African American governor of Louisiana, and several other Black Americans proposed founding a higher education institution "for the education of persons of color" at the 1879 Louisiana Constitutional Convention. On March 7, 1881, the school opened its doors in New Orleans with twelve students. The school grew so big that in 1914 it was relocated to Scotlandville, along Scott's Bluff, facing the Mississippi River, north of Baton Rouge, where there was enough land to accommodate its growth.

What really caught my attention was an article I found about student protests at Southern during the spring of 1960. Sparked by the Woolworth's lunch counter sit-ins by North Carolina A&T University students, students at Southern were arrested for sitting in at first a Kress lunch counter and then at Sitman's lunch counter, and two were arrested for sitting in at the Greyhound bus station. The following day, masses of students walked out of class and marched to the state capitol in Baton Rouge.

Maybe I had chosen the right college to attend after all? If students there were involved in the civil rights movement, I could join them.

As I worked and bought clothes and other items and tried to prepare mentally to leave home for an extended period for the first time, events in the civil rights struggle continued to unfold. I paid close attention. In June, the Student Nonviolent Coordinating Committee and the Congress of Racial Equality, two leading civil rights organizations, organized a campaign called Freedom Summer in Mississippi to attempt to register African Americans to vote. Hundreds of volunteers, Black and White, from different parts of the country, descended upon Mississippi, which was considered the most segregated state in the country.

On June 21, three of those volunteers, Michael Schwerner, James Chaney, and Andrew Goodman, disappeared after being arrested near Philadelphia, Mississippi, and released late at night. For more than six weeks, the nation tuned in to nightly television coverage as the FBI and four hundred Navy sailors searched for them. On August 4, the three men's bodies were discovered. During the investigation it emerged that members of the local Ku Klux Klan and police officials were involved in the brutal murders.

On July 2, two days before Independence Day, the United States Congress passed the landmark civil rights and labor legislation that outlawed discrimination based on race, color, religion, sex, or national origin. It also prohibited unequal application of voter registration requirements, and racial segregation in schools, employment, and public accommodations. Civil rights activists called the law a victory for freedom.

As the date for freshman orientation neared, another important event took place. I and millions of others watched and listened on August 27 as a Black woman from Mississippi spoke to the Credentials Committee at the Democratic Party National Convention held in Atlantic City, New Jersey. The Mississippi delegates to the convention were all White, and Black Mississippians pressed to be included. They had formed their owned delegation, the Mississippi Freedom Democratic Party, and requested they be given four seats in the White Mississippi delegation.

Fannie Lou Hamer was a simple woman, like my mother or Miss Ella Lee, who lived next door. She began working in the fields on a plantation when she was six and had a sixth-grade education. In 1962, she volunteered to work with the Student Nonviolent Coordinating Committee registering Black people to vote. Now she was on national television, advocating for her people. I watched intently as she sat with the microphone in front of her, addressing the credentials committee at the Democratic National Convention and the nation. She told of how she and seventeen others traveled twenty-six miles to the courthouse in Indianola to complete their literacy test. After being confronted by policemen and forced to pay a fine and enduring the grueling trip home, their troubles still weren't over.

> Reverend Jeff Sunny carried me four miles in the rural area where I had worked as a timekeeper and sharecropper for eighteen years. I was met there by my children, who told me the plantation owner was angry because I had gone down—tried to register [to vote].
>
> After they told me, my husband came, and said the plantation owner was raising Cain because I had tried to register. And before he quit talking the plantation owner came and said, "Fannie Lou, do you know—did Pap tell you what I said?"
>
> And I said, "Yes, sir."
>
> He said, "Well I mean that."
>
> Said, "If you don't go down and withdraw your registration, you will have to leave." . . .
>
> I had to leave that same night.
>
> On the tenth of September 1962, sixteen bullets was fired into the home of Mr. and Mrs. Robert Tucker for me. That same night two girls were shot in Ruleville, Mississippi. Also, Mr. Joe McDonald's house was shot in.

I felt sad and proud at the same time. Sad that I, too, understood the pain Fannie Lou Hamer had shared. I felt proud because this unassuming yet dignified woman had, in a profound way, spoken for so many Black people, past and present. Then I got angry. That anger soon turned into determination. I was determined to join the fight, to be a part of the struggle. I went to my bedroom, opened the trunk Madear had bought for me, and began putting more clothes into it. In a few days I would be on my way to Southern University. There I would plunge in, I was thinking, to play my part in destroying this Jim Crow system that had wreaked havoc on my people for too long.

The morning before I was to leave, I was lying across my bed, taking a nap.

"Brother. Papa here to see you," I heard Madear call from the kitchen.

I hurried from the bedroom to meet Papa and his good friend, Mr. Thomas. Both were seated on the sofa.

I smiled when I saw my grandfather. "Hi, Papa. How you, Mr. Thomas?"

"I'm fine." Mr. Thomas just nodded.

"We just wanted to come by to see ya befo' you go tomorrow," Papa told me. "What's the name of the college ya going to?"

"Southern University."

"That's a pretty good piece from here, ain't it?"

"Yes, sir. Over two hundred miles."

"How you gonna git there?" Mr. Thomas asked.

"I'm gonna catch the train in Coushatta."

Papa stretched out his long legs and tapped his foot against the floor.

"Well, it won't be long now. You done us real proud. Real proud."

"Yeah, you sho' is," Mr. Thomas said. "Your granddaddy talk about ya all the time. Don't you, Theodore?"

"He know how proud I is," Papa replied quickly.

"I think you his favorite," continued Mr. Thomas.

"Thomas, I love all my grandchilluns. All of 'em."

"You told me he was your favorite."

"Thomas, you talk too much. Brother, we came by 'cause we wanna give you a little something," Papa said, changing the subject.

Papa reached into his right front pants pocket and pulled a twenty-dollar bill from it and offered it to me.

"Here, take this. I know it ain't much, but maybe it'll help a little. I wish I had more to give ya."

"No, Papa, you don't have to give me anything." I moved a few steps back from him. "I got everything covered. I got scholarships and all. I'm okay."

Papa got up from the sofa. "You take it, now! Take it! I want ya to have it. That's why I'm givin' it to you! Take it."

His strong left hand grasped my right and he placed the twenty-dollar bill into it.

"I want you to have it."

"Thank you, Papa." I pushed the money into my pants pocket. Then Mr. Thomas stepped up.

"I got something for you, too."

He thrust three silver dollar coins into my hand.

"Mr. Thomas, you don't have to do this. You don't have to do this."

Mr. Thomas looked befuddled as he stood there not knowing what to do or say.

"But I came here to give it to ya," he finally blurted out.

"Take it, Brother," Papa told me. "You gonna hurt his feeling. That's what he wanna do. He proud of ya, too."

"Thank you, Mr. Thomas. This will help a lot."

Papa looked at me for a long time. I wondered what he was thinking. I wondered just how tough life had been for him. He had been a sharecropper for most of his life. How much had this aging Black man seen? How many indignities had he endured? I knew he was a proud man, quietly proud sometimes and stubbornly proud at others. How much had that pride been wounded over the years by circumstances he'd felt helpless to confront?

"I'm gonna miss our li'l talks," he said just above a whisper.

"Me, too, Papa. I'm gonna miss them a lot."

Finally, he shook my hand and walked slowly to the door, his head down.

"Papa is leaving," I told Madear.

Madear walked in from the kitchen.

"You be careful, Papa."

"I will, daughter. I will."

Soon he and Mr. Thomas were gone. I would never see my grandfather alive again.

Before my day of departure, I had visits to make, too. I knew that Ma'am Ma would never forgive me if I didn't come to say goodbye. I had to see my older sister before I left, too. And Daddy.

"Just look at ya, boy. Ain't you something?" Ma'am Ma said, greeting me as she stood in front of the ironing board that occupied a lot of her time. A tub full of freshly starched shirts, pants, and dresses sat nearby. Another load of clothes for a White family had to be finished.

"Come over here, boy, and give Grandma a hug. Lord have mercy."

She embraced me tightly and I wondered where this small woman had gotten so much strength.

"Wait right here. I wanna show ya something."

She released me and hurried into another room and returned with a brown album and opened it.

"This some of your hair when you got your first haircut. Here. Look at it."

I held the well-preserved lock of hair in my hand.

"And look at this."

She lifted a small piece of paper from the album.

"This is your first report card, when you was in the first grade. Lurline would have a fit if she knew I had this. Your Ma'am Ma don't throw away nothin'. I even got your first pair of shoes. I got a poem you wrote when you was nine years old."

"How do you keep all of this, Ma'am Ma?"

"I told you I don't throw nothin' away. I got some of the other children's stuff, too."

"I'm gonna miss you, Ma'am Ma."

"I'm gonna miss you, too. But you go on away from here and make something outta yourself. Ain't nothin' here. We did all we could. But you go and do better than what we did. Grandma proud of ya. You'll be the first one to go to college."

"Yes, ma'am."

"I got a box I put together for ya. It's already wrapped. Let me go and get it."

Ma'am Ma returned from the kitchen with a white shoe box wrapped with white cord.

"Just a few goodies to take with you on the train."

We embraced again and when I left, I promised to write her.

"You better come by to see your sister befo' you go," Jurdine told me after she had escorted me into the modest house she and her husband had purchased.

My big sister was a mother four times now, two sons and two daughters. She had gained weight since her lithe teenage years. But she still had her bright face, that bright face that made others comfortable and invited them in. Like Madear, she had become a great cook and was proud of it. I knew she had prepared something for me to take with me.

"Time sho' fly, don't it? It seems like just yesterday that I was teachin' you how to dance. Remember? Sister sho' could dance, couldn't she?"

"Yeah, you sho' could, Jurdine. You used to spin me round so fast, I would almost hit the wall."

"We had some fun, didn't we, Brother? We had a lot of fun."

"Remember when you beat those Joneses when I was in the first grade? You took them all on."

"They made me mad! Nobody mess with my brother."

"You didn't have to beat 'em up that bad."

"Yes, I did. They messed with my brother. Nobody git away with that."

"Well, you certainly showed them."

"I had 'em all runnin' like scared chickens."

We shared a long, hearty laugh that filled the small living room. Then our laughter ended and we both remembered the reason I had come.

"I know Madear don't wanna see you go. Daddy, either."

"Probably not. But I have to. I can't stay here."

"You got that right. Not if you wanna make something out of yourself. You gonna be somebody important. Everybody say that. Sister so proud of you."

"I'm proud of you, too, Jurdine."

"Wait! Wait! I got something for you."

Quickly, she pivoted and hurried to the kitchen, returning with a brown paper bag.

"Sister cooked a pineapple upside-down cake and I put three big slices in this bag. You can eat it while you're on that long train ride. I know Madear gonna cook you something. Madear can really cook, but your sister can hold her own. Let me know how it taste."

She placed the brown bag in my hands.

Jurdine stared at me for a long time. I wondered what she was thinking. Suddenly, she grabbed me, hugged me and wouldn't release the embrace. I could see the tears rolling down her face.

"Look at me crying like a baby," she said, releasing me from her firm hold. "I'm sho' gonna miss you."

"I'm gonna miss you, too."

We smiled at each other for a moment, then I turned to leave. I felt a few tears run down my cheeks, too.

After I reached the yard, my big sister issued her last farewell. "Sister love ya!"

"Love you too, Jurdine."

The parking lot of Winfield Funeral Home, built just a few years before, was filled with cars. I walked past them and opened the glass door of the brick structure and walked inside.

"Hey, Hudson."

The voice stopped me just as I started up the steps to where I thought my father would be. I turned around. It was Mr. Bob Johnson.

"I hear you're leaving tomorrow for Southern University," he continued.

"Yes, sir. I leave in the morning."

"Good. How're you getting there?"

"I'm taking the train in Coushatta."

"You not taking the bus?"

"No, sir. The bus takes several hours longer. It makes too many stops. It goes to all those small towns that nobody ever heard of."

"Well, tell Hud"—that's what he called my father—"he can take tomorrow morning off so he can drive you."

"I will."

"Good luck, now!"

"Thank you."

When I reached the small efficiency apartment that was located on the top floor of the funeral home, my father was sitting on the bed, watching television. He had lived there ever since Mr. Johnson had given him a job at the funeral home. Sometimes, PG and I helped Daddy put up tents at cemeteries to provide shelter for grieving families during funerals.

"Come on in, son," he welcomed me when he saw me standing in the doorway. "Daddy taking a little break here. Have a seat." He pointed to a chair near the bed.

"I just wanted to come by before I leave. I'm heading out in the morning."

Uneasy, he rose from the bed.

"I was gonna come to see ya befo' you left. Ol' Bob got me working my tail off."

Giving him an out, I said, "I know how busy you are."

"So, you ready? You all prepared?"

"I'm ready as I'll ever be."

Daddy then moved to his favorite topic.

"I don't know what's wrong with those Cardinals. They can't seem to make any ground on the Phillies and the Reds. That Lou Brock is something, though. I'm glad they got him. He's knocking the cover off that ball. He's fast as lightning, too."

"You know he's from Southern University."

"He is? They must have a good team, then. You gonna try to play baseball there?"

"No. I'm gonna focus on my studies. I'm not good enough to play on that level."

"Ya never know, son. Why don't ya give it a try?"

"I'll think about it."

"What's that you got there in your hands?"

"It's a package Jurdine gave me."

"She had John drop off several pieces of cake here a few days ago. I ate it so fast."

"She can burn. Well, Daddy, I gotta go. I wanted to drop by before I leave."

"I'm glad you did, son. John gonna take you to the station, ain't he?"

"Yes, he's gonna take me."

For no apparent reason, Daddy picked up the morning paper that covered most of the bed. I guess it gave him something to do during an awkward moment.

"I would take ya, but tomorrow is a full day for me."

To avoid adding to the awkwardness, I didn't tell him what Mr. Johnson had said.

"I'll see you when I come home for Christmas break," I told him.

Daddy stood up. As I stood next to him, I realized how much taller I was, by at least four inches.

"Son, you take care of yourself," he advised me, escorting me to the door. "And you study hard now, you hear. And don't let them girls get into your head."

We both forced a smile. I shook my father's hand and left.

CHAPTER 25

Moving On

The next morning, I heard that booming voice.

"Brother, it's time to get up."

It was Madear.

I scrambled out of bed, PG right behind me. After washing up, I followed the aroma that emanated from the kitchen. Madear had risen early and had already prepared breakfast, her signature large biscuits, sausages, and scrambled eggs. And she had already gotten a plate ready for me. She placed it on the dining room table and pulled out a chair.

"Sit down and eat. You got a big day ahead. Go ahead. Sit down. I know you hungry." She was right. I was hungry. I ate both biscuits, the sausages, and the eggs.

"You want some mo'?"

"Naw, I'm full now."

My mother picked up my empty plate and carried it to the kitchen sink. "What time is John coming?" she asked on the way.

"Nine o'clock," I answered.

PG helped me bring the large green trunk from our bedroom to the living room. It was so heavy, we both struggled with it. My new clothes were inside, along with several pairs of new shoes, sweaters, underwear, sheets, towels, and even bars of soap, based on a list the university had sent. Inside, too, were pages of my writing and unused notebooks.

"You got everything?" Madear asked, opening the trunk that I had not yet locked.

"Why you going into my stuff, Madear? I told you I have everything."

"I'm just double-checking. Ain't nothin' wrong with that."

"Come on, Madear. Suppose I went into your things?"

"I'm the mother and you're the child," she snapped, and closed the trunk.

By now, the entire Hudson household was up and about, but the time seemed to drag before John pulled into the driveway.

"John's out here," one of my brothers yelled from the porch.

I hurried to get one end of the trunk. PG grabbed the other end and we took it to the porch. Madear followed. I knew that look was coming. It was the same look she had had when she stood in the doorway watching PG and me go downtown for the first time. It was that same look when I left to go to Southern to participate in the rally. I would be away from her, outside of her protection, her ability to intercede on my behalf. She knew she and Daddy had raised me well. She knew that I would avoid getting into trouble, despite getting drunk on prom night. It was a mother's worry—no, it was a Black mother's worry for her Black son. It was a worry that was constant in a society where too many White people were determined to destroy and exploit Black people, especially Black men.

"You ready?" John asked after walking to the steps.

"Yeah, I'm ready." I picked up one end of the trunk and PG picked up the other.

"Let me give you a hand," John told PG, and he grabbed the other end. We took it to his car and put it in the trunk. Afterward, I went back to the front porch and approached my mother.

"Well, Madear, it's time for me to get out of here."

I reached to hug her and she embraced me and started crying.

"Madear, you cryin'!" one of the children commented.

"I can't help it! My son is leavin'."

Madear released me and used her apron to wipe away the tears.

"I'll be all right, Madear," I tried to reassure her. "I'll be fine."

"Ain't nothin' gonna happen to him, Miss Lurline," John seconded.

I hugged all my brothers and Lauriece, then slid into the front seat of the car and waited for John. I looked back toward the porch. There, covering the steps, were all my siblings— PG, with whom I had shared so many experiences; Lillo, the trickster of the family, always involved in a prank, he kept us laughing all the time. There were Curtis, the musician, the guitar player, and the budding artist; and Lauriece, the singer, a little Aretha. There were rough-and-tough Raymond and Babebro, the last nearly five years old and trying to find himself. I got a long eyeful of all of them. My family! I was their big brother. I would miss them.

As John pulled off, I saw them all waving frantically.

"Bye, Brother!"

"See ya later!"

"We'll miss ya."

"Send me something when ya git there!" That was Lillo.

I looked at my mother one last time. Still standing on the porch, she pulled the bottom of her apron toward her face again. I knew she was wiping away tears. I would miss that grand old lady. I waved one last time. She waved back and looked as if she was about to run after the car. But it pulled away from that house on Mary Street. It had begun as a three-room shotgun structure. But over the years, with love and children, pain and joy, triumphs and failures, it had become a home.

When we pulled up to the train station in Coushatta, John helped me get my trunk aboard the train. Once I found a seat in the Colored section, I said goodbye to John and watched him walk slowly away.

I sat in a seat near the window. I saw John standing on the

platform, both hands in his pockets, trying to find the window where I was seated. When the train pulled off, he waved and I waved back. Soon, it was thundering down the track.

I finally had my opportunity to get away. To go where it would be different, where there was more to see and to do, where I could join the struggle for freedom, where I could, maybe, become a writer. As I stared out the window, I thought about home again and felt the urge to go back, to go back to the love, the warm safety that home in that segregated town provided. I had the urge!

But I knew that I must push on, push on to find my place, my purpose, my destiny. I would always have Mary Street, the east side, and the people in that Southern town called Mansfield!

CHAPTER 26

Joining the Struggle

"Welcome to Southern University," the dean of students told the more than two thousand curious students on the first day of freshman orientation. Soon, we all would be embarking on our first year as college students.

I embraced the idea of being on my own. Now, I thought, I could make my own decisions, go where I wanted to. At home, my freedom was hampered because Madear and Daddy had the final word. But once the campus rules and regulations were shared with us, it felt as if I was back home again. Administrators told us we couldn't leave campus. We were required to go to church service. All student activities ended at ten o'clock p.m. We weren't allowed to have a car even if we could afford one. Most of the female dormitories were located across a creek and required walking across a bridge to get to them. Campus security guards patrolled the bridge, checking anyone who desired to cross it. I quickly learned the term "in loco parentis," which meant in the place of parents. The university now served as our parents.

My adjustment to college life went smoothly. Charles Johnson, a classmate from DeSoto who had received a scholarship to play basketball, was my roommate. Our dormitory room was tiny, but for the first time I had my own bed, even if it was a small one.

Soon the Southern University campus was bustling with activities. I was among the students who hustled across campus to their classes like colony ants scurrying to and from their nests.

I quickly discovered the university bookstore and the library. I had never seen so many books in my life. There were books about almost everything. Among them were novels, collections of poems, books about Black history and culture, and scholarly books, all written by Black writers. The first day, I just stared at those books, going from section to section in the bookstore. The next day, I went to the library and did the same. I just couldn't believe all those books had been written by Black authors. There were books by Langston Hughes, Richard Wright, Ralph Ellison, Margaret Walker, W.E.B. Du Bois, Gwendolyn Brooks, James Baldwin, Claude McKay, Lerone Bennett, Chancellor Williams, Carter G. Woodson, and John Hope Franklin. I grabbed up a handful, including *Black Boy* by Richard Wright. It was the first book I read through completely without putting it down. I identified with Wright because, like me, he enjoyed writing. And, like me, he wanted answers to the many questions he had, especially answers to questions about White prejudice and racism against Black people. For the first time, I saw myself in a book.

After my introduction to Black literature, I would rarely be seen on campus without a book in my hand. I missed classes as I sat in my dormitory room or in the student center, immersed in a book. Sometimes, inspired by what I was reading, I wrote poems or essays.

I was angry, too. Angry that I didn't have access to these books when I was younger. What if I had read *Black Boy* in elementary school? Or the poetry of Langston Hughes and Gwendolyn Brooks? I realized what impact those books would have had on an inquisitive young boy intent on expressing himself with words on paper. But a school system controlled by mostly White segregationists determined what Black students like me would have to read. I read the only books about Black people I saw in our school library: biographies of George Washington Carver and Booker T. Washington. I think they were part of a series of biographies about famous Americans such as Abraham Lincoln, Thomas Jefferson, and Theodore Roosevelt. They were probably written by White authors.

A few weeks into the semester, I heard applause and cheering as I headed to my dorm room. I rushed to see what was going on.

A large group of students were gathered around a White woman and a Black man who were standing on the base of a statue near the student union building.

"We need volunteers to come with us to do voter registration in Mississippi," the woman told us. "We promise to have you back in time for your classes on Monday. You all know what is going on in the South. We're in a fierce struggle for Black freedom, and we need your help."

"Where are y'all from?" one student asked.

"We're from the Southern Student Organizing Committee."

"You're not talking about SNCC?" asked another student.

Quickly, the Black man who was with the woman stepped up.

"No, we're not SNCC. Our members, both White and Black, come from colleges and universities in the South. We're about the same work that John Lewis and SNCC are involved in. And that is freedom for Black people."

Dressed in blue jeans and a blue denim shirt, the slender, articulate Black man caught my attention. He had a thick mustache and a long beard that he kept pulling on as he spoke. A pack of cigarettes bulged from the pocket of his shirt.

After the two finished their appeal, I wanted to know more.

"Where do you sign up?" I asked.

"We'll be right here on Saturday morning at eight to pick up those who want to join us," the White woman answered. "I'm Kathy. What's your name?"

"Wade," I answered.

I felt uncomfortable. I had never engaged in a friendly conversation with a White woman before.

"This is Herman Carter," Kathy said, pointing to the Black man, who was now puffing on a cigarette he had lit. "We call him Slick."

"What's up?" Slick greeted me.

"Nothing much. So where y'all going on Saturday and what are you doing?"

"We're going to Wilkinson County in Mississippi to try to register Black voters," Slick answered.

I came back to hear them speak again. One day the dean of students made them leave, but they returned the following day.

On Saturday, I officially joined the civil rights movement when a group of us were driven to Wilkinson County in Mississippi to talk with Black people about registering to vote. My first assignment was quite an adventure. Each volunteer was dropped off on long, sometimes isolated dirt roads where the old wooden houses could be fifty to a hundred yards apart. Whenever I saw a car on the lonely road, my heart would pound. Could it be the KKK?

After a successful chat with an elderly Black couple, as I walked back to the road I saw two large dogs following me. Now, to say I was afraid of dogs would be a gross understatement. Dogs terrified me! I began walking at a brisk pace, hoping the dogs wouldn't notice my nervousness. It didn't work. I looked back. The two canines charged at me, barking ferociously. In a split second, I reached my maximum running speed. But the dogs ran, too, and gained on me. When I reached the road, I looked back. They were still charging.

Ahead of me, a barbed wire fence ran parallel to the road. If I could reach that fence and jump it, I thought, the dogs might go away. Still running as fast as I could, my shirttail flying in the wind behind me, I timed my leap as best I could. But it wasn't high enough to clear the nearly four-foot fence.

My left calf landed on one of the barbs of the fence and I felt a sharp pain shoot through my leg as I hit the ground. Still concerned about the dogs, I looked up to see them running back to the house I had just left. The old man had seen what was happening and called them back.

I stood up, still holding the voter registration forms and pen in my left hand. My left pant leg was torn. Blood ran down my uncovered leg. I pulled off my shirt and then my T-shirt and used it to wrap my leg and then continued with my assignment.

I was not deterred by that misadventure. I traveled with the group from SSOC on other voter registration campaigns. I learned as much as I could from Slick. Well read, he talked a lot about Black history and shared some of the books in his personal library with me. Slick was four years older and had been a civil rights worker for more than two years.

As I became more active in the civil rights movement, I once again began to lose interest in my classes. I preferred the books Slick introduced me to, books by Langston Hughes, Richard Wright, James Baldwin, LeRoi Jones, Margaret Walker, Ralph Ellison, and others that I didn't know existed before I got to Southern University. I read those books when I should have been studying and began seeking new books on my own. I always had a book in my hand. This new knowledge inspired me to write down my own ideas. I sometimes wrote two or three poems a day.

During my freshman year, two friends, both named Peter,

joined me on a journey of self-discovery, civil rights, and student involvement.

Peter Jackson had roots in Virginia and Harlem, New York. But he usually claimed Harlem as his home. Harlem was the unofficial capital of Black America and it was where Malcolm X delivered so many of his powerful speeches. Peter was a real campus radical, a paperback book always pushed into the back pocket of his blue jeans and a comb always shoved into his uncombed Afro. Like me, he read as many books as he could. We eventually became roommates, often holding court in the yard for students who wanted to hear new information about Black history and the Black struggle.

During student rallies, students called the university out for not embracing and teaching our history and for its restrictive rules that treated us like children rather than maturing adults. We encouraged the administrators to establish relationships with the Black community across the tracks in Scotlandville, the neighborhood we were told to avoid. I even helped draft a list of demands that led to a protest in the spring of 1967 in which thousands of students blocked entrances to the campus and occupied the administration building.

Peter Johnson was already a veteran of the civil rights movement when I met him. From Plaquemine, Louisiana, he was one of the many youngsters who had participated in the protests there during the fall of 1963, around the same time that the March on Washington took place. The Congress of Racial Equality, one of the four major civil rights organizations during the 1960s, had come to Plaquemine to inspire Black citizens to fight against discrimination. Their efforts were met with a violent response from White citizens and the police. James Farmer, head of CORE, was supposed to be one of the speakers at the March on Washington, but he was in jail in Plaquemine. Since Farmer was a target of the local police and the KKK, supporters had to sneak him out of town in a hearse to save his life. Peter was among the many young people who were the main protesters.

I traveled to civil rights hot spots such as Jonesboro and Bogalusa, Louisiana, where I got to meet the Deacons for Defense and Justice, a group of Black men who organized and armed themselves to protect civil rights workers and members of the Black community from the KKK. They were forerunners of the Black Panther Party for Self-Defense, organized in Oakland, California, in 1966. The Deacons for Defense was founded in 1964 in Jonesboro.

Following the student protests at Southern, in the summer of 1967 Peter Jackson and I left Southern and joined Volunteers in Service to America (VISTA), a national governmental program that placed volunteers, mostly college students, in cities across America to fight poverty. We were assigned to Newark, New Jersey, and arrived there just after the rebellion that lasted from July 12 until July 17. The beating and arrest of a Black cab driver by two White police officers triggered a violent response by Black people that resulted in 26 deaths, 727 injured, and massive property damage. The uprising was just one of more than 150 that erupted across the country during what was called the Long, Hot Summer of 1967. Peter and I participated in the difficult work of helping to rebuild communities and lives that had been devastated during the rebellion and addressing the extreme poverty and racism that confronted Black Newarkers.

That October, I joined more than one hundred thousand mostly young people in Washington, D.C., to protest the Vietnam War. Like so many in the country, I felt that the conflict in Southeast Asia that the United States began to fight more aggressively in 1964 was wrong and that too many people were dying fighting it. Gary Hadnot, one of my high school classmates and a baseball opponent during summer league baseball, had been a casualty of the war. College students, especially those from Black colleges and universities, the poor, and those from working-class families were drafted to fight. It was another example of racial discrimination and inequality in the country.

On April 4, I dropped by the office of the Scholarship, Education, and Defense Fund for Racial Equality in New York City to see Ronnie Moore and Spiver Gordon, two civil rights veterans I knew from my time in Baton Rouge. Ronnie was executive director of the leadership training organization, committed to serving civil rights organizations and producing community leaders. Spiver had come up from the South for a visit. We had been chatting for more than an hour, discussing the direction the movement needed to take.

I began questioning whether the nonviolent tactics used by the civil rights movement were still effective. My struggle-for-freedom baptism had occurred that way. But Stokely

Carmichael's call for "Black Power" resonated with me, as it did for so many others. So did the embrace of Black identity and Black culture and arts. Did achieving our freedom rest with an integrationist approach where we allowed police officials and racist Whites to brutalize us as we marched and picketed? Or did its success depend upon defending ourselves, understanding and appreciating our history and culture, and building our own institutions as articulated by Malcolm X?

Of course, Ronnie and Spiver still believed firmly in the approach they had used so effectively in the South. I, like so many other young Black Americans, felt that this Southern strategy would not work in the North and on the West Coast. Many Black people in these urban areas were forced to live in crowded housing and had fewer employment opportunities than White workers. They faced violence from the police. Some could vote, but it didn't matter, many felt. They felt that turning the other cheek was an unreasonable tactic.

Suddenly, Ronnie motioned for us to quiet down. The television had caught his attention. He rushed over and turned up the volume.

What we heard devastated us.

> Dr. Martin Luther King has been shot by an assassin in Memphis, Tennessee.

The news report didn't say he had been killed. So we prayed that the venerated leader wouldn't die.

Afterward, without thinking, I blurted out, "Now maybe the revolution will come!"

With tears rolling down his face, Spiver started toward me. Ronnie stopped him.

"That youngblood doesn't know what he's saying," Ronnie told Spiver. "He hasn't been where we've been."

"Go on, man! You don't understand the gravity of what has happened. Go and leave us alone," Ronnie shouted at me.

As I walked slowly from the office, I regretted my insensitive remark. I, too, was crushed by the news of this civil rights icon being shot. While I waited for the bus for Newark, I heard someone with tears in their eyes say that Dr. King had died. I made it back to my apartment and stayed there. Meanwhile, unrest erupted across the country. In more than 120 cities over the next ten days Black people expressed their outrage, hurt, and anger.

A few weeks later, while the nation tried to recover from the aftermath of Dr. King's assassination, I headed back to Baton Rouge, where I reunited with Peter Johnson, Leeman Hawkins, and several other friends.

Together, we resumed our community organizing. One day during a telephone conversation with my mother, I was told that Louis Flanigan, a son of Reverend Lud Flanigan, the leading minister in Mansfield, had been convicted of raping a White woman and was sentenced to life in prison. Louis had been the star quarterback for our high school championship football team. After graduating from Grambling College, he became a teacher at a high school in neighboring Shreveport. Now he had become a victim of Southern White justice.

Flanigan's case was a reminder that although I had been involved in civil rights activities and social issues in other cities, I had not done anything in my own hometown.

I told Peter about Louis's case and suggested we go to Mansfield. We might be too late to save Louis, but at least we could confront the system that had railroaded him. Peter made a few calls to headquarters at the Southern Christian Leadership Conference, an organization with which we had been associated. After getting their support—especially that of Ralph Abernathy, the vice president—Peter, Leeman, and I headed for Mansfield. Peter felt strongly that I should not remain there, because my presence could jeopardize the safety of my family and relatives. Reluctantly, I heeded Peter's sound advice and went back to Baton Rouge. For the first time, the civil rights movement had come to Mansfield. The small rural town would never be the same again.

Peter and Leeman helped to organize the movement there. It was young people, however, who were especially mobilized and who led the protests. Flanigan's case dragged on for a few years and he was eventually released from prison.

I learned from my mother that I had received a military draft notice. Certain that it had been prompted by my activism, I was determined not to honor it. At first I planned to report to the induction station and refuse to take the Oath of

Enlistment just as Muhammad Ali had done, but I decided that that wouldn't be the best move. I didn't have Ali's fame. I would be tossed in jail and that would be it. I decided I simply wouldn't report and would wait to see what happened.

Later, when I discovered that the FBI was looking for me in Baton Rouge, I hopped a bus and headed for the San Francisco Bay area of California, the hotbed of activism, the home of the University of California Berkeley free speech and antiwar movements and flower power.

So much happened around the country during those four months I lived in California. In August, thousands of antiwar demonstrators were beaten and arrested by the Chicago police at the National Democratic Convention held in Chicago. In September, Black Panther Party founder Huey P. Newton was convicted of voluntary manslaughter for the killing of a police officer. In October, fifty years before Colin Kaepernick kneeled to protest police violence and systemic racism, Tommie Smith and John Carlos used the Black Power salute as their means of protest at the Summer Olympics held in Mexico City.

In November, Richard Nixon was elected president, providing a major boost to the backlash against civil rights progress. After that, the civil rights movement would not have the same impact in the country. Then, on November 6, one day after the presidential election, a strike at San Francisco State College began that would lead to the establishment of the first Black studies program in the country. Television news programs and newspapers were filled with stories about protests, strikes, unrest, and unfair rulings in court cases.

Most exciting for me, however, was when my brother PG visited in December. He had just gotten out of the Air Force. After enlisting, he had been sent to Vietnam, where he was injured. We hadn't seen each other for more than two years. PG and I spent countless hours reminiscing about our days growing up in Louisiana.

My appearance on a local radio program to talk about my involvement in the civil rights and the Black students' movement in the South was probably what brought me to the attention of the FBI again. When friends informed me that several strange men had been inquiring about me, I knew it had to be the FBI. I was among the thousands of young men who had tried to avoid induction into the military. The firm hand of the government was determined to replenish the supply of men it needed to fight the unpopular war.

Maybe they think I wouldn't go back to Baton Rouge, I thought. So that's where I went. After I returned, I rarely left the apartment an old friend allowed me to share. But one day, two FBI agents knocked on the door.

"Did you receive an induction notice?" one of them asked.

"Induction notice?" I tried to look puzzled. "No, sir, I sure didn't," I lied. "It probably went to my house and my mother didn't know what it was."

I expected to be arrested. Instead, the agents asked me to verify my current address and said another induction notice would be sent to me. I had better respond to that one, I was told, or I would be arrested. A few weeks later I received a notice that directed me to report to the military induction center in New Orleans.

As I rode on the Continental Trailways bus en route to New Orleans, I was frightened. I didn't want to go to Vietnam. If I was inducted, I knew that's where I would be sent. That was where all Black men were sent, it seemed.

I had a plan, but I was afraid it might not work. While I was in Berkeley, several White male students had shared ploys they had used to avoid induction. Pretending to have a mental disorder was one of them. At the induction, I would talk incoherently, even striking another inductee if necessary, to show that I was mentally unfit to serve in the military.

Several hundred young men, Black and White, checked in at the center. During check-in, I complained incessantly, about anything and everything.

"Will you shut up!" one of the military officers yelled at me. But I kept talking.

Soon, we were all directed to line up and told to undress.

As I stood in the nude, staring menacingly at a short White guy next to me, I could see one of the officers staring at me.

"Step out of line," he said. I was directed to put on my clothes again and taken to a small room off to the side. My escort whispered to the other officer seated behind the desk and left.

"So, what is your problem?" the officer asked.

"My problem?"

"Yes. They seem to think you have an issue."

"I don't have an issue," I said.

"Well, they seem to think you do. Sit down over there."

The officer pointed to a chair near his desk. For the next five minutes, he and I talked about sports and books we had read.

Then he said rather abruptly, "You just don't want to go to Vietnam. Well, you got your wish."

I was stunned, so stunned I couldn't say anything. I couldn't even gather the words to show my gratitude.

He gave me a 1-Y classification, a medical deferral, which meant I didn't have to go into the Army. It took all I could muster to keep from shouting hallelujah as I left the room where I had been saved. *Was there a divine intervention?* I wondered.

Back in Baton Rouge, I focused on community organizing. A group of us, including Frank Stewart, a former Peace Corps volunteer who had spent time in countries in Africa, formed SOUL (Society for Opportunity, Unity, and Leadership) in Scotlandville. Frank was chosen as chairman and I was selected to serve as vice-chairman. SOUL incorporated strategies and programs that civil rights organizations and groups like the Black Panther Party employed. Younger members wore berets like the Panthers—ours were red—and we instituted a breakfast program for children, as they had done. But our activities also included registering voters, conducting Black history classes, and setting up and maintaining a portable library.

But what seemed to us to be nonthreatening community activities were apparently major offenses to many White people who were determined to keep their racist, Jim Crow system intact.

CHAPTER 27

Paying the Cost

The two Baton Rouge police officers watched me closely as they escorted me, handcuffed, to a room in the parish jail. As we entered, I saw a large table stationed in the middle. Seated at it was a short brown-skinned man with a receding hairline. When he saw the three of us, he rose. The two officers walked me to the table and then sauntered back to the door and stood there, their eyes still fixed on me.

"Wade Hudson?" the short man asked.

"Yes, sir," I answered.

"I'm Murphy Bell. I'm an attorney. I have been asked to come here to talk with you. Well, to offer my services, if you're open to it."

The name registered with me quickly. Murphy Bell was an important civil rights lawyer in Baton Rouge. I'd first heard his name in 1967. He was one of the attorneys who represented H. Rap Brown, who had replaced Stokely Carmichael

229

as head of SNCC, when Rap was arrested in Cambridge, Maryland, for inciting a riot and carrying a gun across state lines.

"Sit down," he told me.

The handcuffs and leg shackles made it a challenge, but I managed to sit at the table.

"You guys have gotten yourselves into a tough situation, huh?" He sat down again, too.

"Mr. Bell, I don't know what's going on." My look of concern must have been obvious to him. I took a quick look at the two officers, then leaned closer to Mr. Bell.

"All I know is that I heard on the radio that the police had a warrant out on me."

"You turned yourself in, right?" Mr. Bell asked me.

"Yes, sir."

"You haven't talked to anyone?"

"No, sir. Several plainclothes officers talked to me but I didn't tell them anything. I don't know anything," I replied.

"That's good! Don't talk to them. You don't talk to anyone. Now, first off, do you want me to represent you? The judge has assigned you a lawyer, but you don't want that."

"Yes, sir, I want you to be my lawyer. But I don't have any money," I told him.

"Don't worry about that."

Mr. Bell opened his briefcase and pulled out a yellow legal pad and a pen. He positioned the pad neatly in front of him and grabbed the pen and held it firmly.

"You say you don't know anything?" he asked, scribbling a few words on the pad.

"Not that I know of," I replied.

"Well, according to the announcement that the city fathers gave a couple of days ago, you, Frank Stewart, and Alphonse Snedecor are accused of conspiring to murder Mayor Woody Dumas, District Attorney Sargent Pitcher, Plaquemine police chief Dennis Songy, and Eddie Baur, police chief here in Baton Rouge."

"What?!" When I tried to leap to my feet, the shackles reminded me that my movement was hampered.

"I don't know who any of those people are, except Woody Dumas. He's always on television or in the newspaper. They must be out of their heads! Why would we want to kill them?"

"Don't underestimate it, Wade. It's a big story. It's all over the news here, and I believe the national news picked it up, too."

I slumped in my chair and shook my head in disbelief.

"We're going to fight this! Don't get a defeated attitude on me, now," Mr. Bell told me.

"I'm not checking out. This whole thing just seems so unreal, that's all." I looked Mr. Bell straight in the eyes. "What do you want me to do?" I asked.

"For right now, just answer a few questions so I can get an idea of what we're dealing with. Do you know Tiny Tim?"

"Tiny Tim? Yeah, he's that snaggletoothed little dude who hangs around us sometimes. I don't know much about him. He's always trying to talk like a militant. Always talking about the evils of the White man. I stayed away from him because there was something weird about him."

"Well, there was something weird about him. He's a paid police informer!"

"What?" I shook my head. I just couldn't digest all the information I was receiving. "I thought he was too dumb to be a rat for the man. He can hardly put a sentence together."

"He doesn't have to be smart. All he has to do is follow directions. The police say they have tapes of the three of you that Tiny Tim recorded in his car. You know Snedecor was arrested at the railroad tracks just outside Scotlandville with a rifle in his hands," Mr. Bell informed me.

"No, I didn't know that. I haven't talked with anyone."

"His picture, with that gun, was on the front page of the newspaper."

"Oh, God!" I sighed. "Mr. Bell, Alphonse has some problems. I think Vietnam messed him all up. He's like so many of the brothers who have returned from 'Nam. They ain't ready to come back to society."

"Have you had any encounters with Tiny Tim?" he inquired.

"No, not really. He used to hang around us, talking trash. I've never been in his car! Never!" I stopped. "Wait. Just one time. He kept coming into the house asking me to come outside. He said he had something important to tell me. I sat in his car for a few minutes. But I didn't talk about killing anybody. I ain't that crazy. Frank ain't, either. But Alphonse may be different. Mr. Bell, like I told you, Vietnam did a job on him. He is always on edge."

"Well, we'll have to see what evidence they have, however fabricated it is," Mr. Bell said.

"I guess they can get away with railroading us just like they've done to so many other Black folks."

"We'll see what we can do to stop them. I've got to get you out of this place. They got your bail set so damn high. It's one hundred thousand dollars."

"One hundred thousand dollars? One hundred thousand dollars!"

"Relax. Relax. We'll get to work on it."

I tried to relax. I wondered what was happening with SOUL. Were the programs we had started still going to continue?

"I guess you're used to dealing with cases like this, huh?" I asked Mr. Bell.

"Unfortunately," Mr. Bell replied matter-of-factly. He closed his briefcase and the two of us walked to the door where the two officers waited.

"I'll be in touch," he said. He nodded to me, forced a smile, and left. The two officers escorted me back to solitary confinement.

The next day, two plainclothes officers came to my cell.

"You're going with us," one of them told me.

The cell door was opened, and I was handcuffed and escorted out of the building. An unmarked police car awaited us. The two officers didn't say anything. One held a long gun in his hand. I couldn't tell what kind it was, but I kept my eyes on it. The other officer directed me to the back seat of the car and closed the door behind me. Soon we were moving out of the parking lot.

I didn't know where I was being taken. The car moved briskly through the streets of Baton Rouge. From time to time, the officers chatted with each other. But they said nothing to me. After a while, we were on the major street that led to Scotlandville.

Why are they taking me there? I thought. *What are they going to do to me?*

But the officers didn't stop in Scotlandville. The car continued, entering a rural section of the parish south of Scotlandville. There were no buildings, mostly trees, virgin land, and dirt roads. The car turned left onto one of the dirt roads.

My heart sank.

Are they taking me out here to kill me? I thought. *Are they going to say I tried to escape so they had to shoot me?* My mind flashed back to familiar stories about Black people being taken to secluded places where they were killed. Sometimes White policemen did the killing, other times White vigilante groups like the KKK. Was this going to be one of those times?

The car stopped a few yards from the railroad tracks for freight trains.

The two officers got out of the car. The gun-carrying one still held on to his weapon. They stood near the car, talking for a moment. I saw one point to the railroad tracks.

I started praying. I wanted to sing one of those spirituals that gave Madear comfort. But I was afraid it would make the situation worse. So I closed my eyes and continued to pray like I did when I was home at Elizabeth Baptist Church Number Three.

"Get out the car."

I looked up to see one of the officers holding the car door open.

"Get out," he repeated.

I slid out of the car slowly. The officer grabbed me by the arm and led me toward the railroad tracks.

This is it! I thought. I started to pray again.

As the officer escorted me to the tracks, I could see the other one standing in front of the car, still holding his gun.

"Stand here," I was told after reaching the tracks. As I faced the tracks, I closed my eyes, prepared for the inevitable. A few seconds later, I heard several clicking noises that sounded like a camera taking pictures.

I waited, trembling so much my legs felt as if they would buckle.

"Let's go."

I assumed the direction wasn't meant for me. So I didn't move.

"Let's go, I said." This time I couldn't be mistaken. I was being directed.

I turned and saw the officer who had walked me to the tracks standing with a camera in his hand.

That was the sound I heard, I thought. He had taken my picture.

"Go get in the car," he told me.

I walked slowly to the car, wondering if this ordeal was over. Had my prayer worked? I'd thought I was going to be another casualty of the civil rights movement.

During the ride back to jail, I gave thanks to God. I still didn't know why I had been taken to that isolated place. Had the officers expected me to run?

Later, Mr. Bell told me that the picture the officer had taken was probably meant to support their case against me.

"They wanted it to appear that you were giving them information," Mr. Bell said. "From what I'm discovering, they don't seem to have much on you."

I was moved from solitary confinement to a large cell that held ten other men, sometimes more. Late one morning, I was led from the cell to another room in the building. I thought it was curious that I was not handcuffed and shackled as I normally was when I was taken from my cell. I was told to sit at a desk and a document was thrust in front of me.

"What is this?" I asked the officer.

"Just sign," I was told.

"But shouldn't I know what I'm signing?"

"You want to be released, don't you?"

"Released? You mean I'm leaving here?"

I couldn't believe it! Had the committee that had been organized to support us, the Baton Rouge Three, raised enough money to pay my $100,000 bail?

"Did someone pay my bail?" I asked the officer.

"You're lucky," he answered. "You're being released on

your own recognizance. But you ain't going nowhere if you don't sign this paper."

I grabbed the pen in front of me and started to sign. I stopped.

"But I still don't know what I'm signing."

"You're promising to appear in court when you are summoned."

I felt as if the weight of the world had been lifted from my shoulders as I left the room. I had spent twelve days in jail for no reason. Then I got angry. *It wasn't right for them to turn my life upside down like this,* I thought. I was glad to be released. But I shouldn't have been in jail in the first place. And what kind of game were they playing?

As I started to leave the building, I heard someone call my name.

It was Mr. Bell.

"I tried to get here sooner," he said, rushing up to me. "But I had a court case this morning."

"They released me, Mr. Bell!" I told him. "But I don't know why."

"I know," he said, smiling. "I wanted to be here before they did. You didn't have any problems, did you?"

"I don't think so. I had to sign a paper," I answered

"You just agreed to appear in court when they summon you."

"Mr. Bell, what happened? Why did they release me? I'm happy to be out, but I don't know why."

"They didn't do a good job entrapping you, Wade. You were

their weak link. So they dropped the charges they had against you and named you as a material witness. Your bail was reduced to five thousand dollars. But they released you on your own recognizance, which means you don't have to pay."

"Damn, Mr. Bell. These folks don't play, do they?"

Mr. Bell walked with me out of the building. I took in a deep breath of air. Because it was another typical warm Southern spring day, the air wasn't so fresh, but it sure felt good. Then I thought about the other two men who made up what had become the Baton Rouge Three.

"What about Frank and Alphonse?"

"Ben Smith from the ACLU (American Civil Liberties Union) office in New Orleans is Frank's lawyer," Mr. Bell answered. "He's good. Alphonse's family has a local attorney. These White folks are determined to make examples out of you all. This is a big case for them. They have invested a lot into it and they can't move away from it. You're fortunate that Tiny Tim wasn't able to lure you into some of those taped conversations they say they have as evidence. Where are you headed?"

"I'm going to Scotlandville, back to the apartment," I answered.

"I would give you a ride, but I have some other business I have to attend to."

"I can get the bus."

Mr. Bell shook my hand and held it for a long moment.

"I'm glad you're out. Jail isn't a place for anyone to be."

"How can I thank you, Mr. Bell?"

"I'm just doing what I'm supposed to do, Wade. Now, you be careful. Stay away from trouble. They will be looking for any excuse to arrest you again."

"I will. And thank you," I told Mr. Bell as he hurried off.

I walked slowly to the corner of the street to catch the bus that would take me to Scotlandville. I was out of jail, but I had no idea what to expect next.

When the bus arrived, I boarded it, walked to the back, and found a seat.

Fighting for freedom and justice certainly isn't easy, I thought, looking out the window at folks walking the street, going about their daily business. I started thinking about Mansfield and the people I had grown up around. I had a clearer understanding now how difficult fighting for change could be. I now had more sympathy for those people, those generations that came before me and the way of life they had created in order to deal with the racial prejudice and hatred they faced constantly. They had seen family members and friends brutalized and sometimes killed, their property taken away, victimized by the legal and political system. They had seen people they knew leave town to escape the harsh treatment, sometimes escaping to save their lives. I now had a greater appreciation for how they had endured when the odds were stacked against them in almost every way in the general society.

It was in Mansfield where my burning desire to make a difference, to make things better for my family and for my people, had been kindled. That desire still burned. *No matter what obstacles I have to face,* I thought, *I will continue to fight for change, for justice, and for fair treatment for a people I love and care for.* It was that love that made me defiant.

I settled into my seat on the bus and took a much needed rest. A lot of hard work still awaited me.

AFTERWORD

The little Black boy growing up in the small town in northwest Louisiana called Mansfield didn't know much about its history, or the history of the people who lived and worked there.

I didn't know until years later, for example, that Mansfield began as a settlement in 1843 and was officially incorporated in 1848. Just as in much of the South, the area's economic foundation was the institution of slavery. In 1860 in DeSoto Parish, where Mansfield is located, 8,507 African Americans were enslaved to work the fertile land where cotton, corn, and sugarcane grew bountifully. There were only fourteen free people of color who lived there. Some of those enslaved African Americans could have been my ancestors. My mother's father was born in 1895. His father or his mother could have been one of them.

I had never learned this history!

Determined to maintain slavery, eleven Southern states, including Louisiana, seceded from the United States of America after Abraham Lincoln was elected president in November 1860. The Civil War that followed lasted four long, devastating years. The North won, and with its victory came an end to slavery. But Southerners were still determined to retain their system of oppression and control over the lives of Black folks. They enacted laws called Black Codes to prevent African Americans from exercising their rights as citizens.

I didn't know that in 1867, some Republicans who had supported an end to slavery passed federal laws to protect the rights of newly freed African Americans. Union troops were sent to Southern states to enforce those new measures. Under this protection, African Americans saw a new burst of freedom during a period that became known as Reconstruction. They voted; established businesses; built schools, colleges, and churches; bought land; and established farms. Fifteen African Americans served as United States congressional representatives, two as United States senators, and nearly 1,500 served in state and local government offices.

I didn't know that history then.

I didn't know that White Southerners amped up their resistance in their fight to regain control. Vigilante groups like the White League and the Ku Klux Klan wreaked terror and violence against Black people all over the South. In Louisiana, these groups and their supporters were especially vicious. Thousands of Black people were killed.

By 1877, those who had supported African Americans' struggle for freedom had, like the rest of the nation, grown weary of the effort. After Rutherford B. Hayes was elected president, federal troops were removed, allowing Whites to take control of almost all areas of life in the South again. State by state, in towns and cities, laws were passed that firmly established a system of segregation and discrimination called Jim Crow, a name derived from a caricature of Black people made popular by White actor Thomas D. Rice. These laws determined when, where, and how Black people could work. They took their voting rights away, confiscated their land, and controlled where Black people could live and how they could travel. Enforced by wanton violence and murder, these laws established another form of Black servitude that would endure for more than three-quarters of a century.

I didn't know any of that history when I was growing up. I wouldn't find out about it until years later, after I left Mansfield and continued my search for the unobstructed history of the world, through which I had to find my way. Knowing that history, however, helped to explain the town and the world into which I was born. It was a world that had already been constructed for me, had already been shaped for me, just as it had been for my father and my mother.

But in our Black communities, our Black world, despite the hard lives, the discrimination, and the humiliation, folks pushed to find places where they could enjoy loud laughter, sing songs, tell their stories to each other, and just thank God for another day. We had our own businesses. Though most were small, they served the needs of the community. Funeral homes that offered insurance as well as burial services, cafés, dry cleaners, grocery stores, rooming houses, and bars, called juke joints, were scattered throughout our neighborhoods. Churches and schools, however, were our bedrock. Almost every social, cultural, spiritual, and educational activity was held in these irreplaceable institutions.

For most of us youngsters, Black teachers were the first in our communities to influence us, to inspire us. There were few other Black professionals. There were no Black doctors, no Black accountants or Black lawyers. It was said that there was once a Black dentist in Mansfield. But he wasn't there when I was growing up. But there were teachers.

I often watched how teachers conducted themselves—how they spoke, dressed, and talked about the world beyond my humble surroundings. They had gone to colleges such as Grambling, Southern University, and Wiley, historically Black institutions. At the time, I didn't know anyone in my extended family who had gone to college. In fact, few people I knew had ventured outside DeSoto Parish. Those who had, rarely came back. So, I looked up to teachers like Mr. and Mrs. Blow; John Sherman Johnson, my high school homeroom teacher; the fastidious English teacher, Ms. Florence Henderson; and Mrs. Gloria Collins, who taught civics.

Reverend M. B. Collins, the pastor of Elizabeth Baptist Church Number Three, where my family and I were members, was an inspiration for me, too. I was impressed by his quiet strength and oratorical skills. He could preach! I would sit in church, absorbed in sermons that took the congregation on biblical journeys. When he preached about Daniel in the lions' den, I felt I was right there next to Daniel, facing those ferocious lions. When he preached about the Hebrew exodus from Egypt, I closed my eyes and saw myself among the thousands crossing the Red Sea, fleeing the pharaoh's Egyptian army. I guess, without knowing it, the future writer in me was being stimulated by Reverend Collins's ability to engage an audience with the power of his words.

Although not perfect, Black communities in Mansfield were wholesome places where people looked out for each other, especially for the children. Elders were respected and honored. Love floated about and manifested itself in the warm hugs we received, the encouragements that were bestowed on us liberally, and the hot meals that kept those who didn't have much from going hungry.

Jim Crow was meant to cripple, to dehumanize, to destroy us! All the resources that could be mustered were employed to do just that. But the human spirit in Mansfield was imperishable, unconquerable, and could not be contained or legislated away. Love was boundless and perpetual. It wrapped all who were covered by it in comforting and protective embraces. It whispered defiantly these words from a song Curtis Mayfield wrote in 1964: "I've got to keep on pushing."

Stop the love?

No way Jim Crow could do that. No way!

I am a composite of those experiences accumulated while growing up in Mansfield. There were the sweet ones as well as the bitter ones.

The sweet ones helped to encourage me, lifted me up, embraced me, made me feel good about who I am. They covered me with the blanket of love necessary for me to flower.

The negative experiences had their impact, too. The bitter

ones, like segregation, racism, and poverty, sought to over-power the sweet ones.

All of them helped to shape me, to mold me, to make me who I am. They helped to determine my life's path, my resolve to be a part of the change necessary to create a fair and just world for Black people, for all people.

REMEMBERING

Many of the people in Mansfield who impacted my life while I was growing up there are gone now. My father; my mother; my sister Jurdine and her husband, John, and their oldest daughter and youngest son; my brother Wilbert Charles (Lillo); Ma'am Ma; Papa; all of my aunts and uncles; many of my cousins; Bob Johnson; June Henderson; Deacon Walter Taylor; and Uncle Jamie Jones have all joined the ancestors. Gone, too, are some of the Mary Street Boys and those who grew up on the east side—Ray Bogan, Cleonis Henderson, "Crow" Williams, Charles Douglass, Robert Ray Horton, Allen Jenkins, and Li'l Ray Woodley. But time moves on, revealing new ages, new experiences, and new places—if not better ones, at least different. Vida Blue went on to an illustrious baseball career, winning three World Series and a Cy Young Award, and Jesse Hudson played for the New York Mets.

My brothers Curtis, Raymond, and Wilbert and my sister Lauriece established careers as musicians, singers, producers, and songwriters. Curtis wrote "Holiday," the first pop hit for recording star Madonna. Many of the students who graduated with me established professional careers as college professors, school principals, and entrepreneurs. Wanda Faye also had a distinguished career as a school principal. I had an opportunity to speak with her a few times before she passed.

The case against Frank Stewart and Alphonse Snedecor folded when the fabricated evidence and entrapment by the police informer became so evident that everyone could see through it. Yet it took months in jail, an endless number of court appearances, a lot of money, and almost six long years before the charges against Frank and Alphonse were dismissed. Frank was one of those unsung heroes of the civil rights movement. I still think of the quiet, gentle spirit that defined him and directed his interactions with others. Alphonse was one of the many Americans who were tragically impacted by the Vietnam War.

Civil rights friends Peter Johnson and Leeman Hawkins brought the civil rights movement to Mansfield in 1968 and changed the town in many ways. Bob Johnson was one of the local leaders, and meetings and other activities were held at the funeral home he managed. Over the years, Mansfield has had several Black mayors, council members, and other public officials. The current chief of police is Vida Blue's younger sister Annette. Louis Flanigan, who spent almost eight years in prison for a crime he didn't commit, had his conviction overturned in 1975 by the United States District Court.

After leaving Mansfield, in 1969, Peter Johnson moved to Dallas, Texas, where he became a prominent civil rights leader for more than four decades. Leeman currently lives in Denver, Colorado.

Following my arrest in Baton Rouge in 1970, Madear rushed to be there. Despite being afraid because she had never been outside DeSoto Parish, she wouldn't allow anything to keep her from her son when she felt he needed her.

I will never forget the proud look she had when I came back to Mansfield to take her to vote for the first time. Stepping high, her head erect, she approached that voting booth with the same pride she had had when she assumed her post as an usher at Elizabeth Number Three. She rarely missed an opportunity to go to the polls after that.

During the summer of 1971, the other Peter—Peter Jackson—invited me to visit him and his friend Marie in Cambridge, Massachusetts, where he was attending graduate school and Marie was enrolled at Harvard Law School. It was in Cambridge that I met Cheryl Willis, who would become my wife and business partner. Peter established a long career as a college educator, and Marie, now deceased, became a lawyer and a judge in Massachusetts.

In May 1979, DeSoto High School closed its doors when the formerly all-White Mansfield High School was integrated. Today, student enrollment at Mansfield High is 87 percent Black and 7.7 percent White. The once all-White high school is now essentially Black.

When school board officials proposed razing the school buildings of DeSoto High, an alumni association was organized and it rushed in to save them. The buildings now function as a community center, carrying on the legacy of the pioneers who fought tenaciously to provide educational opportunities in Mansfield and to lift the Black community in the most difficult and challenging times.

I now know much more about Indigenous people and their role and influence in Louisiana. The Caddo people once occupied most of the territory where Mansfield, DeSoto Parish, and the surrounding area are located. Many towns, cities, bodies of water, and even schools bear the names of words from languages of Indigenous people who populated the state of Louisiana before Europeans came. They include the Houma, Natchitoches, Opelousas, Coushatta, Jena, Ponchatoula, Powhattan, Avoyelles, Caddo, Catahoula, Calcasieu, Tangipahoa, Ouachita, and Tensas.

I participated in the civil rights movement and the student movement of the 1960s, and I continued to write. I have written many books for young readers as well as plays. In 1988 Cheryl and I established a publishing company called Just Us Books, which publishes books for children and young adults, the kinds of books I wished I had had when I was growing up in Mansfield. I have accomplished some of the dreams that little boy had.

Still, the struggle for Black equality and justice goes on in all areas of American society. Cheryl and I started Just Us Books because of the disparity of books for children and young adults that spotlight Black culture, Black history, and Black experiences. An old axiom of the civil rights movement that helped to nurture me in so many ways still applies. It simply declares: THE STRUGGLE CONTINUES. . . .

NOTES

The **Period of Reconstruction** (1865-1877) took place in the southern United States following the end of the Civil War in 1865. The era included the impeachment of a president, outbreaks of racial violence against newly freed African Americans, and the passage of constitutional amendments and other legislation addressing the status of African Americans. During this period, African Americans were elected to political offices at national, state, and local levels. It also included Union troops being stationed throughout the South to protect African Americans and to help enforce laws.

During the 1870s, a few years after the Civil War ended, a codified system of segregation and discrimination was instituted in the United States, especially in the South. Called **Jim Crow Laws,** these statutes affected almost every aspect of daily life, mandating the segregation of schools, parks, libraries, drinking fountains, restrooms, buses, trains, and restaurants based on race.

Sharecropping was an agricultural labor system used throughout the South after Reconstruction ended in the 1870s. To address the lack of free labor that slavery once provided, many former plantation owners hired mostly Black laborers to work their crops in exchange for a share. They provided housing for the workers—usually a mere shack—and credit to purchase food and supplies from a store typically owned by the landowner. Because workers rarely earned enough money to pay what they owed, they were bound to the land perpetually. Many saw this as another form of slavery.

Southern University and Agricultural & Mechanical College began in 1880 as the result of a movement to establish institutions of higher learning for Blacks in Louisiana. Originally located in New Orleans, it was later reorganized and became a land-grant college, and in 1914 the school was moved to Scotlandville, a community north of Baton Rouge. There were very few Black residents in Scotlandville in 1914 when the Louisiana State Legislature purchased more than five hundred acres on Scott's Bluff, overlooking the Mississippi River, to be the site of Southern. When a Standard Oil refinery moved there in 1909, the area had begun to industrialize, and following World War I, Black people began migrating there from other parts of the state. Eventually, Scotlandville became the largest majority Black community in Louisiana. The railroad track that we crossed was a dividing line separating the college campus from the town. But in so many ways, the two were mutually dependent.

Black schools have always been inadequately funded by school systems. That was especially true during the decades of the early 1900s. Black Americans often had to build and support their own schools. In 1917, the **Julius Rosenwald Fund,** established by the president of Sears, Roebuck & Co., stepped up to help. Over several decades, the fund contributed to the construction of over 5,357 school buildings, nearly 200 teachers' homes, 163 workshops, and 5 industrial high schools for African Americans, with a combined pupil capacity of 663,615 students, mostly in Southern states. A friend of civil rights leader and educator Booker T. Washington, Rosenwald was inspired to support the education of Black children after reading Washington's book *Up from Slavery.* Local citizens donated land and labor that were matched by financial contributions from the fund. Some Rosenwald Schools still stand today and are used as community centers; some have been designated as historic sites.

World War II was the biggest and deadliest war in history. More than fifty countries engaged in combat in every continent except Antarctica. More than 75 million people died in the war, including 40 million civilians. Nazi Germany's invasion of Poland in 1939 precipitated the conflict, which lasted for six years and ended when the Allies defeated Nazi Germany and Japan in 1945. The United States entered the war in 1941 when Japan bombed Pearl Harbor in Hawaii.

Black Americans have always fought against slavery, racism, and unequal treatment in the United States. The **modern civil rights movement** was one of those struggles. The *Brown v. Board of Education of Topeka* (Kansas) court decision in 1954, which rendered racial segregation in public schools unconstitutional, is believed by some historians to be the beginning of the movement, and the assassination of Dr. Martin Luther King Jr. in 1968 is considered the end.

During the 1960s, the **women's movement** sought to raise consciousness about the role of women in society. It was focused on what was called women's liberation, including the freedom to pursue roles other than those of wife and mother, the desire not to be regarded as sex objects, and the right to earn equal pay.

One of the most important victories of the modern civil rights movement was the **Civil Rights Act of 1964.** Signed by President Lyndon B. Johnson, the legislation outlawed discrimination based on race, color, religion, sex, or national origin. It also prohibited unequal application of voter registration requirements and racial segregation in schools, employment, and public accommodations. When the bill came before the Senate for debate, eighteen southern Democratic Senators and one Republican tried to block its passage with a filibuster.

SOURCES

Page 45: Principal Dewitt Johnson's quote

https://africanamericanhighschoolsinlouisianabefore1970.files.word
press.com/2017/12/desoto-high-10-02-2017.pdf Pages 7–8 of
the selected pages of the uploaded documents. Pages 19–20 of
the original pages.

Page 167: Alex Haley's interview of Malcolm X in Playboy *magazine*

unix-ag.uni-kl.de/~moritz/Archive/malcolmx/malcolmx.playboy.pdf

*Pages 196–197: Fannie Lou Hamer's speech at the 1964 Democratic
National Convention Credentials Committee meeting*

americanradioworks.publicradio.org/features/sayitplain/flhamer
.html

americanrhetoric.com/speeches/fannielouhamercredentials
committee.htm

*Page 258: Muhammad Ali quote: "I ain't got no quarrel with those
Vietcong."*

si.com/boxing/2020/04/28/this-day-sports-history-muhammad-ali
-refuses-induction-army-stripped-title

TIMELINE

April 15, 1947 Jackie Robinson becomes the first Black ballplayer in the modern era to play major league baseball.

October 3, 1949 WERD, in Atlanta, Georgia, the first Black-owned radio station in the United States, begins broadcasting.

September 22, 1950 Ralph J. Bunche wins the Nobel Peace Prize for his work as a mediator in Palestine. He is the first African American ever to win the prize.

1952 The fear of the polio epidemic reaches its peak in the United States. In 1916, an official announcement had declared polio to be an epidemic in the United States. During the following decades, thousands, mostly children, were killed or crippled by the disease. A vaccine developed by Dr. Jonas Salk was announced in 1955, and by 1979 the virus had been eliminated.

May 17, 1954 In *Brown v. Board of Education of Topeka*, the Supreme Court rules that school segregation at all levels is unconstitutional.

December 1, 1955 Rosa Parks, recognized as the "Mother of the Civil Rights Movement," refuses to give up her seat on a Montgomery, Alabama, bus.

December 5, 1955 African Americans begin a boycott of the Montgomery bus system that continues until shortly after December 20, 1956, when the United States Supreme Court outlaws bus segregation in the city.

February 14, 1957 The Southern Christian Leadership Conference is formed with Dr. Martin Luther King Jr. as president.

August 29, 1957 Congress passes a voting rights act, the first major civil rights legislation in more than seventy-five years.

September 4, 1957 A mob of belligerent Whites prevents nine Black students from entering Central High School in Little Rock, Arkansas.

October 4, 1957 The Soviet Union launches the satellite Sputnik, beginning the space race.

February 1, 1960 A sit-in in Greensboro, North Carolina, initiates a wave of similar protests throughout the South.

April 15–17, 1960 The Student Nonviolent Coordinating Committee is founded in Raleigh, North Carolina.

April 3, 1963 Under the leadership of Dr. Martin Luther King Jr., African Americans begin a campaign against discrimination in Birmingham.

June–August 1963 Civil rights protests take place in many major urban areas.

June 12, 1963 Civil rights leader Medgar Evers is assassinated at his Jackson, Mississippi, home.

August 28, 1963 The March on Washington, the largest civil rights demonstration ever, is held. Dr. Martin Luther King Jr. delivers his "I Have a Dream" speech.

September 15, 1963 Four African American girls are killed when nineteen sticks of dynamite are detonated by White supremacists on the east side of the 16th Street Baptist Church in Birmingham, Alabama. Many other church members were also injured. It took nearly forty years to bring two of the murderers to justice.

November 22, 1963 President John F. Kennedy is assassinated in Dallas, Texas.

January 23, 1964 The Twenty-Fourth Amendment, which prohibits both Congress and states from requiring the payment of a poll tax or other types of tax for citizens to exercise their right to vote, is ratified. Some Southern states had maintained poll taxes as a way to keep Black Americans from voting.

February 24, 1964 Cassius Clay defeats Sonny Liston to win the world heavyweight title in boxing. Clay later changes his name to Muhammad Ali.

March 8, 1964 Malcolm X announces his split from Elijah Muhammad's Nation of Islam.

April 13, 1964 Sidney Poitier becomes the first Black American to win an Academy Award for Best Actor.

July 2, 1964 President Lyndon B. Johnson signs the Civil Rights Act of 1964.

July 18–August 30, 1964 Beginning in Harlem, New York City, a wave of racial conflicts occurs in cities across the country.

February 21, 1965 Malcolm X is assassinated at the Audubon Ballroom in Harlem.

March 7, 1965 Six hundred marchers protesting Black voter suppression and the murder of civil rights worker Jimmie Lee Jackson by an Alabama state trooper are brutally attacked by local police as they try to cross the Edmund Pettus Bridge in Selma, Alabama. Led by civil rights leaders John Lewis and Hosea Williams, the march became known as Bloody Sunday because of the violence inflicted on the protesters.

August 6, 1965 President Lyndon B. Johnson signs the Voting Rights Act of 1965 to protect the right of Black Americans to vote.

October 1966 The Black Panther Party is organized in Oakland, California, by Bobby Seale and Huey P. Newton.

April 28, 1967 Muhammad Ali refuses to be inducted into the U.S. Armed Forces, saying "I ain't got no quarrel with those Vietcong."

July 12–July 17, 1967 A rebellion in Newark, New Jersey, results in twenty-six dead, hundreds injured, and $10 million in property damage. Newark is one of more than 150 cities to experience uprisings during what is dubbed the Long, Hot Summer of 1967.

April 4, 1968 Dr. Martin Luther King Jr. is assassinated in Memphis, Tennessee, by James Earl Ray.

August 1968 Musician James Brown releases "Say It Loud—I'm Black and I'm Proud."

October 16, 1968 Tommie Smith and John Carlos give black-gloved Black power salutes to protest racism in the United States during the playing of "The Star-Spangled Banner" at the Olympic Games in Mexico City.

ABOUT THE AUTHOR

WADE HUDSON is an author, a publisher, and the president and CEO of Just Us Books, Inc., an independent publisher of books for children and young adults. He has published over thirty books, including the anthologies *We Rise, We Resist, We Raise Our Voices,* which received four starred reviews; *The Talk,* which earned four starred reviews and was a *New York Times* Best Book of the Year; and most recently, *Recognize!: An Anthology Honoring and Amplifying Black Life.* These powerful collections were co-edited with his wife, Cheryl Willis Hudson.

Defiant is Wade's homage to the Black people he knew in Mansfield, Louisiana, as much as it is his story about growing up there. These were the people who nurtured and loved him even as they fought for their own survival under Jim Crow. It is also the story of a youngster trying to find meaning and purpose in a defining era when issues such as civil rights, women's rights, immigrant rights, and resistance against the Vietnam War played out regularly on the news. It is about finding one's voice and joining the fight for justice and equality.

Wade lives in East Orange, New Jersey, with his wife.

wadehudson-authorpublisher.com

justusbooks.com